I am for
Black Excellence
The Black Excellence Project
Celebrating local Black history and student voice

The Black Excellence Project and "BEP @ Bard"
is brought to you by the partnership and collaboration of
Amateka College Prep and Bard Early College D.C.
Both of these organizations are at the service of
Washington, D.C. students and families
to escalate academic and social success.

To learn more about bringing
The Black Excellence Project
to your public high school community, contact:
Connect@AmatekaCollegePrep.org

Not a health pandemic,
Not a social pandemic,
could defy your commitment to
justice and equity.

This book is dedicated to the teachers of The Black Excellence
Project for their tireless commitment and outstanding example.
You are each, indeed, for Black Excellence.

Gabriel Morden-Snipper and Roseanna Goseanna, Ph.D.
Mathematics Faculty, Bard Early College D.C.

Mack Scott, Ph.D. and Derek O'Leary, Ph.D.
Social Sciences Faculty, Bard Early College D.C.

Acknowledgments

The 2020-21 program was funded in part by a grant from HumanitiesDC, an affiliate of the National Endowment for the Humanities, with special thanks to Andrea Carroll McNeil, Sarah Imboden and Bard College

Phillip Michael Wilder and
McCarthey Dressman Education Foundation

Book Cover designed by Amber Ravenscroft

Forward.

Our children are watching. Don't they deserve to be inspired? Won't they benefit from learning from role models? Does it not matter to take what they learn in their classrooms and directly connect it to their daily lives? Shouldn't their learning include, inspire and reflect who they are?

The absence of Black Excellence in what we learn in schools is criminal. It robs students of learning from their own communities, examples throughout history and their families and neighbors. We can't exclude the existence of Black people as contributors to society and expect students to know what stories have been stolen from them.

Our students have demanded and demonstrated how they will be groomed for excellence themselves. They have called upon local Black exemplars who have modeled for them what it means to use their lives and careers to end racism. Without often having this exposure earlier in their studies, there are multiple debates and tensions within these pages: should the "b" in Black be capitalized? What is Black Excellence and where should it be taught? Who should teach it? Should it fall on the shoulders of Black teachers or all educators? Do they get to learn about it in the history or English Language Arts classes or all subjects?

These young authors have dared us to fairly include positive representations of Black persons in their writing. They describe how their society will be impacted once Black peoples are positively included in what they learn at school. For additional measure authors in our 2020 edition have chosen to return for this publication in 2021. Others have examined Black Excellence in History, where it is most expected and pushed new ground for learning in Geometry. The ninth and tenth grade students authored in this book clearly see the value of their education including Black role models, across subjects. The bravery of a multiracial, multicultural set of educators was invited and expected and the four instructors in this year's program took the charge to bring in not only Black Excellence within their classrooms, but community perspectives and most importantly, student voice. Their reflections are included in these pages as well. Finally, of the many community members interviewed and studied, one particular role model was standout and is named in many of the essays which follow. LaRuby May truly and deeply inspired our students to pursue racial justice as they learned of her authentic story. They've included May's narrative in their reflections.

In the pages that follow, we hope you are inspired, listening and ready to take the charge to truly be *for Black Excellence.*

Forward Together.
Cassandra "Dr. Cass" St. Vil
Founding CEO, Amateka College Prep &
Founding History Teacher and
Director of The Black Excellence Project, Bard Early College D.C.

TABLE OF CONTENTS

Community Interviews

A major focus of The Black Excellence Project is to recognize and local celebrate Black professionals in their work to end racism. We spent months and many lessons digging up essays and biographies of Black professionals in D.C.'s present and past. We exploded the idea that Black Excellence could only be investigated in the Humanities by expanding this work in mathematics. We studied professionals across a variety of sectors and disciplines, including law, public service, literature, the arts, sciences and more. We explored their professional achievements, and also their personal narratives, introducing many new names we have never been exposed to before.

Many of these untold stories would appear in our classrooms, but the larger goal was to connect students to Black Excellence in their own communities. Learning these stories in class was not enough; we wanted to use the classroom of learning that the entire city offered. In this book edition, community interviews were added so students could pair their classroom studies with their city's history and culture. Throughout this project, students would interview and learn from family members, neighbors, and residents in Washington, D.C. (or who have spent considerable time dedicated to this city).

With the ongoing COVID-19 pandemic, students would interview only those that they could safely interact with. Nonetheless, students kept this mission of community engagement alive by also researching stories about Black professionals from the Greater D.C. area that they hadn't learned in class, including business leaders, organization founders and public figures to learn more about. These student authors then wrote the narratives of this exemplars to share with you in these pages.

We encourage the readers of this book to do the very same that these young authors did: You may come across the name of an example of Black Excellence that you have not heard previously. You, too, can be for Black Excellence by learning more about this role model's impact, research and share their story.

BLACK EXCELLENCE IN MATHEMATICS

Let's Get Even
Mya Martin

In her lecture, LaRuby May discusses the intersection of race and mathematics. She details how living in a predominantly white area, combined with a lack of representation, affected not only the people around LaRuby, but herself. This shortage of people of color within the math realm induces prejudice, where one is likely to subconsciously exclude minorities from the subject altogether simply due to bias. It becomes less expected that minorities are capable of excelling in mathematics and thus even people of color see themselves as not ideal for the role of, say, a mathematician or a lawyer. Even LaRuby, who was able to persist past her own bias found herself in a constant battle to be the best so that she would not be cast aside and her efforts would be noticed.

Black excellence can be described as any example of a feat reached by a Black person despite any racial barriers in the way. In terms of math, Black excellence would be any instance where a Black person achieves a math-related feat despite racial obstacles along the way. As LaRuby mentions, many minorities do not pursue math related careers due to the fact that they don't feel included within the subject. When people of color excel in math and get recognized to high heavens, it inspires other minorities to at least attempt the same. I myself, a Black woman, feel a bit more noticed and safe when I see people with my skin complexion in positions similar to that of LaRuby's.

I have not yet accomplished many feats in math, but when I do, I feel a sense of pride just knowing that my accomplishments were likely directly influenced by a Black person before me, and that I will be indirectly influencing Black children down the line. It is a cycle of Black excellence in my eyes. Representation breeds diversity, which puts an end to racism in the long run. A single person of color within the math realm can incite enormous progress in making mathematics an inclusive subject. But it all starts with acknowledging these minorities and giving them a much-needed spotlight.

Discrimination in Mathematics
Mikalah Ray

Racism and discrimination were big during LaRuby May's childhood and there was only so much that she could do to stop it, but she learned to cope with it and learned different techniques to push through so she could be the best that she could be. During her childhood, she attended an interracial school that still had experiences of racism during the school year. She was a really smart girl, and because she was so smart she was put in an advanced math class where there really weren't a lot of African American students in her class. Because she was so smart and an African American student, she experienced name calling and racist comments during class. She knew that she was one of the few African Americans in that class and that she would experience these things. She tried her hardest to prove these people wrong and show them that she was none of those names that they were calling her, that in fact she was more than what they were calling her. She knew that she was a smart and intelligent young lady who had big dreams in life and wanted to make something out of herself as a Black woman.

When I heard Ms. LaRuby May's experience being a Black girl growing up, there was something that I could relate to also being a young Black girl. I can understand her drive to prove others wrong when they doubt your intelligence. But now, in the time that we live in, fortunately some of us don't have to experience those racist comments and slurs that she might have been called as a child. Knowing that that is what those young Black children had to go through during that time makes me look at life differently. It makes me more grateful for all the laws and acts that have been passed to combat racism. I am thankful because I could not imagine going through what Ms. May went through. Hearing her story touched me because it taught me more about what those young Black children had to go through on top of trying to stay focused in school.

What Black excellence in mathematics means to me is Black people showing that they are good at many things in life, and that one of those things may be mathematics. To me, it is a Black person proving others wrong and showing that they can do the math and all the hard work that may come with it. It is important to do these things because in this world now Black people are being doubted in life and told that they could never be good at anything. We need to prove those people wrong, and make others proud, and show that we can do these things, that we can be someone great in life by doing these things that we are good at. Just like LaRuby May was told that she couldn't be good at math and she was doubted at her talent. But she showed Black excellence and proved those people wrong. Now she is a Black scholar who other children may look up to as a role model. Because she showed that it is possible to be someone in life that can do something great with their life, it influenced others to do the same. So it is really important that you show your Black excellence because you may never know who you may influence or help on the journey of becoming the best person you can be.

Black Excellence in Mathematics
Dionne Hill

LaRuby May grew up living in the South. During LaRuby's interview, she talks about how she was the only Black African American in her entire middle school. She talked about how sometimes it would be hard for her to get used to things. When going to school, her mother would have to encourage her to be strong and to always keep her head up. LaRuby also talked about how during her math class, people would say mean things to her. There was an incident with LaRuby and her classmate in which he basically told her that she doesn't belong in that class. Just listening to LaRuby's stories and the things she went through was very hard, but she turned out to be a successful woman. If I was to put myself in LaRuby shoes, it would also be hard for me. Till this day, we Black African Americans still go through racism. Racism is something that will never end no matter what - it's sad but it's also true. Growing up, I've learned that we as Black African Americans will always be targeted because of our skin color, but we will never give up.

Black Excellence means to have a big impact on the Black community. Black Excellence means to be a role model or make history in the Black community. Black Excellence is very important because we can learn a lot from it. We people of color have been through a lot and for us to have role models and people who made a big difference in the Black community means a lot. I learn about Black Excellence from my parents, elders, and even social media. I feel as though Black Excellence should be taught in every subject. In school, we learn about things that don't matter. In subjects like math and science, Black Excellence should be celebrated by talking about the first creators of those fields, and who created what. I feel like that would be very good for us to learn and to appreciate Black Excellence.

If we celebrated Black Excellence it would change a lot of people's perspectives on the Black community. I feel like we don't acknowledge the black community like we should, and that's a problem. I do feel like schools do not teach us a lot about the meaning of Black Excellence and that's a root of the problem. Black Excellence needs to be acknowledged, even more so with everything going on during this time.

A Local Example of Black Excellence
Adonias Stuckey

Racism and discrimination has had a big impact on the field of mathematics and has created barriers for African Americans and people of color. In her interview, Ms. LaRuby May talked about multiple topics related to racism, including her experience, how to stay motivated, and lack of representation. Lack of representation is among the most important because it is affected by all of the others. Many African Americans don't see a Black inspiration and often they are told they can't achieve something. They can't defend against that opinion if they haven't seen someone like them achieve what they want to achieve. This causes them to lose motivation and the lack of motivation can cause the person to give up. Through all of that, the people that give are the people that would have made the lack of representation not as prevalent and young people of color would gain motivation. It is an endless cycle and unless the cycle is broken, it may hold children and young people back from their aspirations and dreams.

It only takes that one person to persevere and fight through oppression to in the end help break the barrier. Ms.LaRuby is a great example of that person and of Black Excellence. She faced racism as a child in school. She found ways to cope with the oppression and stay motivated, and even "was the first Black president of the student government at [her] school." This is an example of her breaking barriers - she said that being the president helped her to cope because it helped her feel like she was on the same level as the white people in her school. The students in her school were led by her and that made her feel like she achieved something.

A prime example of oppression is the fact that in 2008, America had the first Black president ever in the history of the land. In 1789 231 years ago, we had the first president of the United States of America. In 1619, 401 years ago the first African arrived in America. That doesn't add up - Africans arrived in America 389 years before the first Black president and the first president was 219 years before the first Black president? Why was it made so hard and why did it take so long for an African American to become president?

Sources:
https://www.usatoday.com/story/news/investigations/2019/02/08/1619-african-arrival-virginia/2740468002/

https://www.whitehouse.gov/about-the-white-house/presidents/george-washington/#:~:text=On%20April%2030%2C%201789%2C%20George,President%20of%20the%20United%20States.

https://dcps.instructure.com/courses/195061/assignments/2840257

BLACK EXCELLENCE IN HISTORY

Essay Guidelines

Write at least one paragraph each to answer the following guiding questions about Black Excellence:

1. **What does Black Excellence mean to you?**
   - Why is it important to learn about Black Excellence?
   - Do you believe it is important to learn in schools? Why or why not?
     - Where, other than school, do you learn about Black Excellence?
   - *How* do you want to learn about it at school?
     - Should it only be taught in certain subjects? For instance, should it only be learned in history class?
     - What would you expect in math and science to celebrate Black Excellence?
2. **Who is an example of Black Excellence?**
   - Choose anyone that we learned about at school. This can include individuals we studied or people you know (teachers, family members, coaches, etc.).
     - What are the most significant aspects about this professional's background?
     - What is their professional pathway?
     - How did they use their career to fight racism?
     - Why are they an example of Black excellence?
3. **Who else is an example of Black Excellence?**
   - Choose anyone we didn't get to learn about. This can be an individual or group of people (i.e. Michelle Obama, Regina Hall or Black scientists)
     - Who else would you want to learn more about? Why does it matter to learn about this individual or group?
     - How are they an example of Black Excellence?
4. **Are you "*for* Black Excellence"?**
   - How do you (or, will you) show your support of Black Excellence?

In your conclusion, please address:

   - How would school or life overall change if we celebrated Black Excellence?

What does Black Excellence mean to you?

Who is an example of Black Excellence?

Who else is an example of Black Excellence?

Are you *"for* Black Excellence?" How do you show your support of Black Excellence?

How would school or life overall change if we celebrated Black Excellence?

The Extraordinary Power of African Americans
Author: Amira V. Jones

Black excellence is people of color doing extraordinary things. It is important to learn about black excellence because there are many misconceptions behind the black community that would never be there if people educated themselves about the black community. It is important to learn about black excellence because there are many great things that blacks have accomplished. You should be able to learn about black excellence everywhere you go, not just at school. While in school, black excellence should be taught in all grade levels every year because there will always be something new that we will do every year. It should mainly be taught in history and ELA but it could be used in math and science by using black names in their problems instead of Mark, Sam, John.

A great example of black excellence would be Benjamin Banneker. Benjamin Banneker was born on November 9, 1731. He was born in Baltimore County, Maryland. He was the son of an African slave named Robert, who had bought his own freedom, and of Mary Banneky, who was the daughter of an Englishwoman and a free African slave, meaning that they were legally freed but still forced to work with little to no pay. Benjamin grew up on his father's farm with three sisters. He was a free African-American almanac author, surveyor, landowner, and farmer who had knowledge of mathematics and natural history. His significant accomplishments include the successful prediction of a solar eclipse, publishing his own almanac, and the surveying of Washington, D.C although unfortunately, many of his original papers were destroyed in a fire. Banneker overcame obstacles such as isolation, very little education, and racial descrimination towards him. He became a symbol of racial equality in the abolitionist movement that gave other African Americans the urge to move forward and fight for what they think is right. Though Banneker lived a great and powerful life, all was brought to an end on October 9, 1806. He passed away at the age of 74.

Kevin Durant is an example of black excellence because he shows that he is hardworking and pushes to his goals no matter how many setbacks come his way he will keep pushing and trying to find his way to the top. Kevin also uses his fame in a good way. He says many inspiring quotes that help keep people moving forward. One of his famous quotes states,"So many people doubted me. They motivated me every single day to be who I am." This quote alone motivates me to keep my eyes on the prize and nothing else. Kevin has faced racist comments and treated them like they were nothing. For instance, the host of Fox News, Laura Ingraham, told LeBron James and Kevin Durant to "shut up and dribble" rather than share their views about President Trump as they had in a recent joint interview. Instead of Kevin Durant getting mad and saying something that he may regret, he dealt with this issue in the most responsible way. While Ingraham would later put out a statement claiming there was "no racial intent" behind her words, Durant simply doesn't agree."To me, it was racist," he told USA TODAY Sports while shaking his head. Following that interview he put it past him and his team won his next game. This goes to show that Durant doesn't let anything get between him and his goals. He inspires young men to go past their limits and show that they are more than just lazy kids but they are athletes at heart.

If we celebrated black excellence schools would be better off and there wouldn't be poor education. Everything would be more equal. The celebration of black excellence would change life overall because we wouldn't have to fear the police, we wouldn't have to struggle to get into a good college, and we wouldn't have to struggle to find a good job.

The study of black excellence would change these things because there will be no judging on first glance and getting into good colleges would be based on grades and not your name.

I am for Black Excellence. I always push people forward to be their best selves. I believe that blacks need to work together and not against each other because, to be honest, all we have is each other. I show that I support Black Excellence because I always try to see the good in us and look past the stereotypes.

Uplift The Community We Are All We Have
By Darjae Lucas

What Black excellence means to me is when an individual is succeeding in whatever profession or activity there is, uplifting their community. The reason this is important is because this show's that the individual not only thinks about themselves but their community as well. And when an individual gives back to their community. It is widely appreciated and inspires others to be like them. Another reason why this is important is that Black children need to know that people that are their skin tone can make it. We are the future, but the past can and should help guide the way.

Taraji P. Henson is an exceptional example of Black excellence. I say this because she is a great actress. She has starred in at least 45 movies and shows such as empire, Baby Boy, and Proud Mary. She has also been nominated and won many awards such as Golden Globe Award for Best Actress, B.E.T for Best Actress, NAACP Image Award for Outstanding Actress in a Drama Series, etc. And she uplifts her community by advocating for mental health support. Henson provides mental health support for underserved communities. She created the Boris Lawrence Henson Foundation in 2018 that has provided resources to thousands of people who are struggling. Which is very beneficial to the Black mental health community. I say this because African Americans are 20% more likely to experience mental health problems than the general population, according to the Anxiety and Depression Association of America's (ADAA). And this can be due to African Americans having economic uncertainty, publicized killings of African Americans, and other racial traumas and stressors.

Sister Souljah is another exceptional example of Black excellence. She had written many great books such as *The*

Coldest Winter Ever or *Midnight The Gangster Love Story*. Sister Souljah has been in the house of representatives and has won many honors. Sister Souljah has also made music songs like Harder than you think or fight the power. She is also an African American activist who fought against police brutality, miseducation in urban areas, and racially motivated crimes. As a community activist, Sister Souljah organized several service programs and events. In 1985, she developed and funded the African Youth Survival Camp for children of homeless families. It is a six-week summer sleep-away camp in Enfield, North Carolina. Sister Souljah was also an executive director of Daddy's House. Daddy's House Social Programs is a foundation established in 1994 in New York City that aimed at education, recreation, and sustenance for underprivileged urban youth. The foundation holds classes in all academic disciplines, life-management skills, college preparation, computers, manhood, and womanhood training. These people get presented with opportunities that would have never come if not for the foundation.

I am absolutely for Black excellence. I say this because when youths see more examples of Black excellence. They aspire to be more, and they can have role models to take on their journeys. I show support for Black excellence in many ways. I support Black excellence by giving thanks to those who are examples of Black excellence. That can include supporting Black-owned programs, listening to their music, downloading it, watching movies and shows. And I can show support by buying from Black-owned brands and giving honest good reviews when I can. There are so many ways to support Black excellence.

School and overall life would change if we celebrated Black Excellence in many ways. We would probably have more conversions about Black people showing Black excellence in and out of school. Also, I feel that Black on Black crime would decrease. I say this because African

Americans will see there infinite ways to get money and that crime can be optional. And when people do not have to risk having to get incarcerated, they will not.

28

What does Black Excellence mean to me?
Dionne Hill

What does Black Excellence mean to me? Black Excellence means a lot to me. Black excellence means to have a big impact on the Black community. Black Excellence means to be a role model or make history in the black community. Black Excellence is very important because we can learn a lot from it. We colored people have been through a lot and for us to have role models and people who made a big difference in the Black community means a lot. I learn about Black Excellence from my parents, elders, and even social media. I feel as though Black Excellence should be taught in every subject. In school, we learn about things that don't matter. In subjects like math and science, Black Excellence should be celebrated by talking about the first creators and who created what. I feel like that would be very good for us to learn and to appreciate Black Excellence.

Dorothy Height is an example of Black Excellence. Dorothy Height was a leader in addressing the rights of both women and African Americans as the president of the National Council of Negro Women. Growing up Dorothy always wanted to be an African American Black activist. Dorthy spent her life fighting for civil rights and women's rights. In the 1990s, she drew young people into her cause in the war against drugs, illiteracy, and unemployment. Dorothy's name became very big in the Black community. Dorothy is a big part of Black Excellence.

Michelle Obama is another example of Black Excellence. Michelle has become a big role model to many people. When she became the first black lady of the United States of America it made a big impact on the Black community. Michelle has done a lot of great things for the black community. To this day Michelle Obama will always be a great part of Black Excellence.

So I have a business and the way I show my support for Black Excellence is by supporting other black-owned businesses. When I see other young black entrepreneurs it makes me very happy. During this whole pandemic, I've seen so many black kings and queens start businesses and that's amazing that we're all independent and dedicated. I want to see everybody win and become successful. I love to see these hard-working black entrepreneurs, we are making history.

I feel like if we celebrated Black Excellence it would change a lot of people's perspectives on the black community. I feel like we don't acknowledge the black community as we should and that's a problem honestly. I do feel like schools do not teach us a lot about the meaning of Black Excellence and that's a big problem. Black excellence needs to be acknowledged more especially with everything going during this time.

Black Excellence My Perspective of A Vision
By: Kennedi Green

Black excellence to me means to show people out of our culture that regardless of our skin color, or how less fortunate we are, we still can do great things and be just as smart, helpful, or creative. Black excellence should mean everything to our culture even though it is not heavily taught throughout schools. A lot of things that we use today or the things we may pass on a daily such as buildings, school, and also our homes were built by the community of Black Excellence and I feel as though those small but equally as important tasks like that go unnoticed without showing appreciation towards our culture. I believe that we should learn more about Black excellence because it is an important subject in our history, some do not like this subject not only because they may feel as though we're asking for too much credit, or because other races may feel like this is a competition when this is not the case. I've learned about black excellence from my great, great, great grandmother and also my aunt and they make sure to remind me of how the story went when it came to our history. Even though some teachers may believe it is a tough subject to talk about we need to, this is not only a valuable part of history that the black community is missing but other communities as well. My family believed that it was important to learn about Black excellence because as black males and females we deserved to learn about our culture not only the bad but also the good.

Kevin Durant was born to two government workers, Wayne and Wanda Pratt, on September 29th of 1988. His father's departure before his son's first birthday left Kevin, and his three siblings, to be raised by his mother and grandmother,

Barbara. Kevin grew up in a neighborhood that was 95 percent black and with 80 percent of the people living in poverty. When his father left before he turned one, Kevin and his siblings joined the 67 percent of people from his community that were raised in a single-parent household. The system set Kevin up to fail but he believed in himself, set a goal, and worked hard to reach it. Regardless of him being set to fail or being raised in a place with poverty he strived and believed in himself then he set that goal and worked hard to reach it. Kevin is an outstanding example of Black Excellence because he showed not only he could set a goal and reach it but also he fought the system.

Another person who was an example of black excellence is Jackie Robinson; he was born on January 31, 1919, and died on October 24, 1972, In Cairo, North Stanford which is in the northwest corner of Santa Clara County, California, United States. He moved to Honolulu, Hawaii, where he played football for the semi-professional Honolulu Bears which was soon to be cut short when the United States entered into World War II. During boot camp at Fort Hood, Texas, Robinson was arrested and court-martialed in 1944 for refusing to give up his seat and move to the back of a segregated bus. But Robinson's excellent background, combined with the good reports from good friends, and lastly the NAACP and various Black newspapers, shed public light on the injustice. After his discharge from the Army in 1944, Robinson began to play baseball professionally. He joined the all-white Montreal Royals, a farm team for the Brooklyn Dodgers, in 1946. His ecstatic year led to his promotion to join the Dodgers. Robinson played his first game at Ebbets Field for the Brooklyn Dodgers on April 15, 1947, making history as the first Black athlete to play Major League Baseball in the 20th century. Robinson is a great example of Black excellence because even after being arrested and the racial abuse he still was able to not only fight for his dream but also show we can do great things because we are talented.

I will always show support towards Black excellence not only because it is a part of the Black community but because there is so much more we must learn about our history by supporting Black business and doing right not only to myself but for others as well. I know with each year
passing year and my age growing, I know that there will always be more things to learn when it comes to black excellence and I will look forward to that and not only would this be good for the Black culture but hopefully this subject will encourage others to learn about their history and the importance of as well.

Black Excellence
Raziya Jackson

Black Excellence is African American people striving to be their best selves. It is people that go above and beyond for what they believe in. They work hard for what they want in life and are examples for others. Black Excellence is being a leader and being yourself. It is important to learn to be excellent to make a difference in society.

Educating people on how far black people have come shows what can be accomplished when you work hard and follow your dreams. I started learning about Black Excellence at a very young age. My family taught me to love God, be respectful, and do what I love. I feel like Black Excellence is important and kids should start learning about it young so they can have more knowledge about who they are and who they can be. Black people come from royalty and we should be taught that so we could act like it.

Someone I think is a good example of Black Excellence is my grandfather, Willam Henry Jackson Bey. He's my dad's father. My grandfather, unfortunately, passed away before I could meet him. His accomplishments have been talked about by many. He was the president of the Woodson-Banneker-Jackson-Bey Division #330 Universal Negro Improvement Associations and African Communities League (UNIA-AL). This organization was founded by Marcus Mosiah Garvey and stood on the principles of Determination, Perseverance, and Resilience. Its motto is "One God, One Aim, and One Destiny". The Woodson-Banneker-Jackson-Bey Division is named after Carter G. Woodson who was the founder of Black History Month, Benjamin Banneker who was an inventor and contributor to the construction of Washington,

D.C, and my grandfather Willam Jackson-Bey, who was the respected president of Division 330 until he passed.

My grandfather assisted the District Commissioner for DC, Maryland, and Virginia with starting a new division in Virginia called the Prosser-Truth Division 436. The Prosser-Truth Division 436 got its authorization the day before he died. He studied the legacies of African ancestry and their gifts. He was a prominent adviser in the nationalist community for 25 years plus. He liked to attend many community projects that dealt with the District of Columbia. He made it his job to feed the homeless and one of his greatest joys was giving bread to the community. My grandfather educated other black people on how to be self-reliant. He was strict on knowledge and education. Even though he is not here with us physically, his legacy to be black and excellent will forever live on. (https://www.uniadivision330.org/home)

I believe in Black Excellence because I am Black and Black people are great. I believe everyone should always work hard to achieve their goals. I educate myself on information that I don't know. For example, I did not know my grandfather was the president of the Woodson-Banneker-Jackson-Bey Division. I think about what my ancestors went through for me so I try my best to stay focused and be all that I can be. I will continue to learn about Black Excellence so that I can teach others. I feel like school or life, in general, will change if we celebrate Black Excellence and give credit to what black people accomplish. There are things black people have contributed to the world that we still use today.

Black Excellence Is Key

Black excellence is the action of showing the greatness and power of black people. Since slavery, black people have not been recognized as much as they deserve. Black people have created so much. They have influenced so many traditions and movements and, they have not gotten the credit. Such as, the popularity of Black food culture, our different hairstyles, medical advancements, or even contributing to ending slavery. But Black Excellence helps increase the amount of knowledge about all the great things that black people do.

For instance, think about Kelly Miller. When he was a child, a minister noticed his passion for math and signed him up for the Fairfield Institute. From then, he was outstanding and earned a scholarship to Howard University. After he had graduated, he became the first black man to be admitted to study at John Hopkins University, therefore proving his influence of black excellence. After his days of learning, he decided to become a sociology professor and, he was the first sociology teacher ever at Howard. His impact as a teacher went beyond the classroom and opened a pathway for an addition to his career. While being a professor, Miller created a book called **Race Adjustment**, which discussed his political and social views on the world and African American people. In the book, Miller stated, *"This race has been looked upon as an inanimate mass to be exploited and controlled according to the interest or caprice of the white lord of creation. But the growing self-knowledge and self-assertion on the part of the awakening race can add a new element to the problem that can no longer be ignored."* This means that black people have been oppressed because people thought that their purpose was to be worked to death and used. But a new birth of knowledge had become known, and people couldn't ignore the problem of racism. He was suggesting that it needed to be fixed as soon as possible. So if anyone can portray the title of black excellence, it would be Kelly Miller.

Dominique Dawes is a very famous African American female gymnast. She was six years old when she started gymnastics. By the time she was nine, she was already finding a way to motivate herself to keep going. That was a key element to her success because she is a representative of black excellence. Dawes was the first African American to win an individual Olympic medal in gymnastics. Besides her career, she was a motivational speaker to youth. She let them know her struggles and how to get past them. For example, one struggle that she recognized was her being devastated because she had been hoping to win an individual gold medal. She stepped out of bounds and fell during her floor routine, placing her out of medal contention during the all-around competition. Even after that, she kept pushing and moving forward. She showed children that they needed to have faith amongst themselves and persevere through any struggles in their lives. Dawes taught them about positivity in life. She used her accomplishments and made them useful to society by giving advice and becoming a great BLACK influencer by showing black kids that you can do anything you put your mind to.

I am for Black Excellence because I embody an example of black excellence. My name is Zamaya Givons. I am 14 years old, African American. I have had a 4.0 GPA ever since I was in school. I have never gotten a grade on a report card that was less than a B. This can impact my life heavily because I plan to go to college. I plan on becoming someone great. So if I continue to go down this path, getting a scholarship will be one of the main things coming to me. My entire life I have been striving to be successful and intelligent to show everyone how great and beautiful a black girl could be. This will help me be an example of black excellence because I have hope. I know that I will do big things as I live on in my life. That makes me a person that can inspire people. A person that does the best that they can in life. I also plan on showing support by being the best example of black excellence that I can be. I plan on uplifting and encouraging other black women, men, boys, and girls. So overall, I am and will always be for black excellence.

The overall effect on school and life based on if we celebrated Black excellence would be huge. More people would be respected and congratulated for what they do and who they are. Racial profiling in school systems would not be as much of a thing if more people understood the importance of black people and everything they can do. More kids would grow up to learn the importance of hard work. For example, imagine a young black girl growing up in poverty. Seeing a powerful, intelligent, and determined black woman might encourage her or inspire her to do great things with her life and this is also true for males. If Black excellence was projected into the media as much as racial injustice against blacks, I feel as though our community would thrive off of the positivity and greatness of our people. Our people inspire others to be great. Young African American kids must know about what they can be capable of. Other races must know our importance as well.

-Zamaya Givons

Black Excellence Project
Destiny Clay

Black excellence means flourishing as an individual and being able to inspire other people by their good deeds and actions. Black excellence means to succeed financially, relationship-wise, health-wise, and intellectually. Black excellence also means to grow as an individual and to improve yourself. It is about portraying the great qualities and abilities of Black people and making your family and the Black community proud. It is not only about being a wealthy person but appreciating all that you are given. Black excellence is about setting goals and achieving accomplishments. I believe that Black excellence can be described as an African- American person who holds significance for the achievements they have attained. It is about realizing that it won't always be an easy journey, but with hard work and dedication, one can accomplish their goals.

Charles Richard Drew is a great example of Black excellence. Charles Richard Drew was born on June 3, 1904. Charles was an African-American physician and grew up in Washington, D.C. Drew was the oldest out of all his siblings. "He completed his bachelor's degree at Amherst in 1926. He then decided that he wanted to attend medical school. Unfortunately, he didn't have enough money to afford medical school. He later decided to work as a biology teacher and coach for Morgan College. When he finally had enough money to attend medical school he began pursuing his dream of becoming a brain surgeon. One major accomplishment Mr. Drew achieved was that he was the first to create a blood bank and he also managed two of the largest blood banks during World War II. Drew passed on April 1, 1950." One example of racism that Charles experienced was when a white doctor refused to give him a blood transfusion while he was in the hospital. Even though Charles Drew didn't survive this incident, his legacy will forever be known. He will always be known as the creator of blood banks. When others thought he wouldn't succeed he proved them wrong. In 1944, Drew was officially awarded the Spingarn Medal, the highest honor of the National Association for the Advancement of Colored People.

Actress Taraji P. Henson is another example of Black excellence. Henson played in the film "The Best of Enemies" that deals with the topic of racism. She plays Ann Atwater, an outspoken civil rights activist. "During the racially charged summer of 1971, Atwater and Ellis came together to co-chair a community summit on the desegregation of schools in Durham, N.C. The ensuing debate and battle soon lead to surprising revelations that change both of their lives forever." Taraji acts in movies that deal with real-world issues and she usually plays the main character in those films. She won 15 awards throughout her career and has a net worth of about $16 million or more. Her parents were divorced when Taraji was two years old. But, she still made the best out of her life and is known for her Black Excellence worldwide.

I support Black Excellence. I can support Black excellence by supporting Black-owned businesses and honoring historical figures such as Maya Angelou and Muhammed Ali. I can support Black excellence by being dedicated to my education and spreading awareness about the challenges that Black people are facing today such as inequality, police brutality, poverty, and education funding. The media often doesn't cover topics related to the oppression that Blacks have faced and currently face. Black people have faced for so many years, including being assaulted, mistreated, abused, and discriminated against. These unknown stories and traumatizing experiences have not yet been told by the media and are still being kept in the shadows.

Schools would change dramatically if we celebrated Black Excellence. If more educational institutions taught Black excellence then students would be more likely to form more educated opinions and views affecting our nation today. Scholars would know more about successful African-Americans that have excelled and supported Black communities. Scholars would not only know about the famous activists that the media often portrays, such as Rosa Parks and Martin Luther King Jr, but they would also know about many other influential Black figures. If we celebrated Black excellence all the time, the month of February would not only be dedicated to learning about Black history and Black excellence but each and every school day would be dedicated to learning about it. That way, children can inform others and spread the word to educate people about Black culture, Black history, and influential Black figures.

BLACK EXCELLENCE IN GEOMETRY

Christian Cunningham
Mr. Morden
Geometry
13 December 2020

Black Excellence In Mathematics

The issue I will be discussing will be the lack of representation in many fields of work and research. LaRuby May talked about how, as city councilmember, she had partnerships with Black engineers to have a STEM program at an elementary school for young girls of color during the summer. Though I've never been in the STEM program I have done similar things meant to bring light to new topics and ideas for young people of color. For example, in elementary school I participated in a Geography program of sorts in which we learned countries, cities and states and then went to competition. An experience close to this was one of which I had the chance to travel to a different country based on an essay I wrote, it also being a competitive environment that both opened my eyes to how vast and amazing the world is. So to continue to my point these experiences I believe are not as accessible to children of color especially Black children as they are in other places. The work Ms.May is doing has the potential to open a whole new world to these children leading them to possibilities they've never thought of before. Much like the experiences I've been through all it takes is space that opens other ideas and possibilities for fields of work and study.

Black Excellence in mathematics is the culmination of discoveries and practices made by and used by Black mathematicians. The amount of leaps and bounds made by Black people in mathematics or in other fields with the use of mathematics is history altering. For example, the amazing mathematician Katherine Johnson, whose calculations heavily aided in the first successful crewed spaceflights. The importance of not only Black Excellence in mathematics but the valuing and supporting of Black people in these fields stems from the lack of full and proper recognition. The advancements and breaking of technological, scientific and mathematical barriers made by Black people, even the taking or complete ignorance of those achievements has been happening for hundreds of years and even continuing now.

Karin Bishop
Mr. Morden
Black Excellence in Mathematics
December 13, 2020

Black Excellence in Mathematics

As LaRuby May said in her interview, the reason she was getting frustrated at herself was because she couldn't get the math and she couldn't understand why. She didn't have anyone to help her when it came to math so that even made her frustration worse. But even though she had no one that could help, her parents supported her and told her she was great although she didn't feel like it. She also explained that even though math may seem threatening, you shouldn't be afraid of it because there is a beauty in it and it is used in daily life. Managing frustration in mathematics is hard for me and probably for lots of other students. For me in math class, I get frustrated when I know exactly how to do a problem but it just doesn't resonate with my mind when it comes time for me to practice on my own. For instance, when I just learned a skill I get upset when in class we go over how to complete the problem but I still get it wrong. I understand I might be moving too fast and don't give myself time to think, but it still just gets me upset.

Black Excellence in mathematics basically means having more Black people being represented within the math community. It is important to have Black mathematical figures because it's not that common for Black students to be interested in math. It isn't talked about, it isn't considered fun, and people say you don't need it in life. It isn't usual for a Black student to say "I want to become a math teacher." It is also important to have black figures in math because younger Black students aren't encouraged to take on math. Black students believe math is a white person's subject because all they see are white math teachers. They believe that math isn't going to be a way for them to support themselves or their families. If we have more Black people appreciating mathematics and representing it then it will open the door for more young students to be intrigued with math and want to learn it.

Black Excellence and Me
London Haynie

Have you ever wondered about the term Black Excellence? If you have, what about in relation to mathematics? Mathematics has been drawn back to the Greeks and Europeans, but who should really receive the credit for developing these ideas? This topic was explored in a very educational interview with Black lawyer LaRuby May.

LaRuby May discussed the topic of the lack of representation in the mathematics field. She mentioned how young Black girls had to be especially exposed to mathematics and STEM programs due to the subpar levels of representation, diversity, and exposure in those areas. As a young Black woman, I feel that I should have the same rights to any form of education I choose to pursue, no matter my race. My White peers should not be viewed as more intelligent or more capable to do math. If Black students are treated with the same unbiased education as White students, they can and will be just as good, even if they are not naturally great at math. LaRuby May also mentioned how the lack of representation in math fields can affect younger generations. Racism in this field can cause young Black people to have no role models that look like them to give them hope to carry out the same education and careers. She feels that if Black students had more Black role models who were represented in this field, they would feel more encouraged to also take part in the love for mathematics.

Math is one of the many things that has a lack of representation of Black people. Black Excellence is important because we use math everyday. Whether we realise it or not, math is in everything, from the measurements of the coffee you drink to the length of your shoe laces. This makes math essential to our lives in the simplest ways. In math, the success of Black people should be highlighted because of the lack of credit and stereotypical barriers that have been created over the course of history, outlining Black people as lesser or undereducated. Therefore, when a Black person has a major accomplishment in math or STEM of any kind, it should be celebrated as well as uplifted to show every person of color that where you started does not define where you are going and that you should always follow your dreams. Black Excellence in math is important and will surely aid in the success or recognition of more Black individuals.

In conclusion, LaRuby May's interview taught me many things about how to push past racism in every career field and to strive to be the best. I also learned about many of her personal experiences with racism and the lack of representation in her own field of law. Black Excellence is important in mathematics and deserves recognition. We should not pass around unearned privilege. Hopefully, the disproportionate levels of representation in the mathematics field and other fields will soon even out and improve greatly.

Jailynn Brown
Mr. Morden
Geometry 10
December 13, 2020

The Proof is in the Pudding

Frustration in math classes is something that everyone has faced at some point, no doubt. Math is all about numbers and logic, and some feel that they just aren't "cut out" for it. Councilwoman LaRuby May was naturally good at math, but even so, there were numerous times where she got frustrated while completing her homework. She was frustrated with her lack of understanding, the fact that no one around her was able to help her, and that she was the only African-American student (or one of few) in her schools for many years. But with affirmations from her parents, hard work, and the motivation of securing financial stability for her family, she worked through her frustration and grew to love math.

I really sympathized with this story, because although I am pretty good at math, it often makes me anxious and aggravated. I remember that I had a lot of trouble with math until I transferred schools in first grade. We were learning how to add and subtract in school. I was struggling with subtraction, so my mother took me to Dollar Tree and got me some workbooks. I flew through the addition one easily, and she, my father and my grandmother worked with me through the subtraction one every day after school until I finally got the hang of it. After that, I gained some confidence in my math classes (until seventh and eighth grade). I was really unmotivated in math until last year. But ever since ninth grade, I have been motivated simply by a desire to learn.

Black Excellence in mathematics is every display of a black person even attempting to do a math problem. The act of simply trying to work it out is excellent to me. Black excellence in any subject is a very broad topic, though. In mathematics, it includes black people trying to solve a problem, constructing a building, being a scientist, or making new discoveries in math. Black excellence in math is important because math generally translates to whiteness, and people of African descent don't really have a lot of representation in the subject. Seeing examples of Balck excellence in math will likely empower students to add to the legacy.

Black Excellence In Mathematics
Alaunee Pitts

LaRuby May talked about how when it comes to picking classes, we would prefer to go to dance or art class rather than taking math. We would rather take those classes because we tend to struggle with math and it becomes too much pressure on us when we try to do the work and it's hard. We would rather go to a class that doesn't take a lot of concentration. She also stated that because we are from a certain area doesn't make us less than to achieve a certain goal and understand the concept of the work. In order for us to understand, we just need guidance and to believe in ourselves. For me, mathematics can be stressful but it is one of my favorite subjects. In elementary school, I wasn't good at it at all and I never really understood what was going on because of the way they taught us. Once I got to middle school, my 6th grade teacher helped me understand and I improved so much in math even though I was behind. My 8th grade and 9th grade teachers also helped me understand math really well and now I enjoy going to the class.

Black Excellence in mathematics is being able to achieve and accomplish math, which is one of the most difficult subjects we have. It's also getting help or studying to understand the subject. Black Excellence is important because math is a very stressful subject and to be able to accomplish it you have to be determined. Math is also very important and something we use every day.

Black Excellence Project
Annua Ast-Ra

LaRuby May explained how where she grew up was very racist and how she was the only Black person in her class and how being the only person of color in a class of white people made her feel like the odd one out. I can connect to that because in a way, I've been in a situation where I'm clearly seen as different from others. The way she coped with it was making black empowerment groups to show that people of color aren't only just good for sports. She was able to prevent those stereotypes from falling on her. However she also coped through her religion.

What Black Excellence means in mathematics is that not selling yourself short to what society sees you as. No matter what your skin color is, you can accomplish just as much as the next person. In the movie Hidden Figures, all the white people doubted that these black women could do math as well as them only because of all the stereotypes about how much black women can achieve. However, it is important because it gives other people of color inspiration to look into math and really understand how mathematics is important just to learn. It gives people of color the courage to go into fields nobody even expected they'd be in, and where they don't settle for their limitations.

Black Excellence
~saMARa winston

Black excellence to me is progression; it's saying look at what we have done, look at what we accomplished in a system that was originally built against us. It's so we can see ourselves succeed and to keep us striving for success. Unlike white people, we don't see too many like us succeed in fields that historically we were excluded from. I believe that Black excellence is showing that we can succeed at everything that we do and we don't have to stay in the same places that we are told we are allowed.

It's not weird to think black people and math. There are Black inventors and scientists and they need math. So it's not surprising for there to be Black mathematicians. If Black people were largely associated with anything it would be sports and the arts, acting, writing music, etc. I think it's what society told us we could do, and it's the only thing history acknowledges us for. But I think the reason why I think that Black and math aren't seen together is because Black and smart aren't correlated and Black and logic are not correlated. Historically speaking, the reason we are associated with the arts and sports is because of slavery. Slaves were required to do physical labor. Therefore we had to be good at physical activity. But not only were we required to be strong we also needed to stay in high spirits and to do that we sang spirituals, spirituals were used to convey messages and keep hope alive. As slaves we stayed alive by our own creativity and strength and during the Harlem Renaissance we showed the full extent of our creative prowess, from art to music to writing and we were somewhat celebrated for it opening doors in those industries that were usually closed.

I feel like the wealthier and more educated a black person is, the less they see people who look like them. I live in the gentrified part of Capitol Hill, and my family is the only black people in the whole condo. Most of the black kids I knew from middle school didn't live in gentrified D.C. I went to a fairly mixed middle school with some Black kids, some white kids and other minorities. While we had plenty of smart Black kids, the white kids always were seen as smarter and more trusted than the Black ones. The white kids barely got into trouble, only getting a slap on the wrist at most. I didn't know them personally, but from what I gathered, if you're outwardly smart and well-liked by teachers, you're seen as white-washed, less than or looking down on the others. I think being smart being correlated with whiteness hurts Black children cause it makes them feel less than, because they don't feel Black enough and makes certain people the target of bullying for showing whiteness. During my high school search I visited special private schools, and I felt weird and out of place because I barely saw a Black face. But that's what it's like with higher education: the higher you go the less people you see look like you. It's something you learn very early on if you want extra stuff you have to compromise with money or working harder.

Ay'Maya Murchison
Mr.Morden
Math
12/10/2020

"Underestimated"
The Black Excellence Project- Math Version

LaRuby May spoke on how she was the only Black girl in her classroom, and she explained how that made her feel as being frowned upon when it came time to answer questions or take tests. Teachers or students did not believe in her very much. She seemed like a non-factor in her school surrounded by white people. Yet, the drive and motivation she had shielded the negativity; sometimes it was hard, but she kept proving them wrong. Making good grades and being an athlete and showing she was working to be the first generation to go to college and show them times are different now.

In my opinion there is no such thing as Black excellence in math. You shouldn't have to stand out more because you are Black. A white person should not look at you as excellent just because you're doing well in math they should not doubt you or discriminate from the start. This is important because it shows we need to change the concept of Black people not being able to do certain things. Yes you can be successful in math, but it's deeper than that. Every achievement shouldn't be glorified as if we were doubted from the very beginning.

BLACK EXCELLENCE IN U.S. HISTORY

The Black Excellence Project, as I understand it, is about giving students the space, resources, and support to revise long-standing narratives about what Black history is—and will be.

By writing, our students demonstrate that American history can be reexamined and revised, and that by sharing their voices they can have an influence on its future.

I feel confident that we have a rising generation of students ready to do this,
which I find truly excellent.

-Dr. O'Leary

Derek O'Leary, Ph.D.
History of the Americas &
Social Sciences Faculty

One benefit of teaching American history is that I can ask students questions to which I don't know the answer myself. (*What exactly caused the American Revolution? Has the U.S. fulfilled the ideals of the Declaration of Independence? Etc.*) Whether they know it or not, students are teachers too. After four months of learning with Bard DC's remarkable 9th and 10th-grade students through the Black Excellence Project in our History of the Americas class, I'll attempt my own answer to the central question that our students have explored in such varied and insightful ways: *What is Black excellence?*

From my vantage point, Black excellence is the courage, resilience, and discernment to challenge and revise the narratives that have demeaned and disadvantaged Black Americans throughout American colonial and national history. From the seventeenth century until our day, dominant narratives about Black history and Black Americans have often been like a barricade on the path toward a nation of racial justice and equality. These narratives have justified injustices and obscured the major contributions that Black Americans have made to our history. Narratives can constrain, but they can also empower. In this sense, The Black Excellence Project is crucial work, because by collaboratively reinterpreting our nation's history we can better understand our present and reimagine the future that we hope to live into.

One person who we studied this semester, Phillis Wheatley, was born free in the mid-1700s in West Africa. She was enslaved, brought westward on the Middle Passage, and sold to a Boston household where, in bondage, she learned to read and write. Wheatley became a poet, publishing in 1773 the first book of poetry by an African American in the Western Hemisphere. In one of these poems, she links the injustice of her own enslavement with the American colonists' opposition to the injustice of British rule:

> I, young in life, by seeming cruel fate
> Was snatch'd from Afric's fancy'd happy seat:
> What pangs excruciating must molest,
> What sorrows labour in my parent's breast?
> ...
> Such, such my case. And can I then but pray
> Others may never feel tyrannic sway?

By the American Revolution, Wheatley was widely known in the North American colonies that would soon become the United States. But many could not accept that an African American woman was capable of producing such powerful poetry. Others diminished it, even if it was hers, as inferior. In his famous *Notes on the State of Virginia* (1785), future president Thomas Jefferson degraded her work, concluding that, "the compositions published under her name are below the dignity of criticism." Jefferson's misconceptions and prejudice blinded him to the extraordinary poetry that was in front of his eyes; his narrative denying African Americans' artistic potential prevented him from seeing Wheatley as she was, and all of this enabled his defense of the indefensible institution of slavery.

The Black Excellence Project, as I understand it, is about giving students the space, resources, and support to revise long-standing narratives about what Black history is—and will be. This means reassessing the nation's past, but it also means reimagining its present and future. In itself, a five-paragraph essay by a Bard DC student can seem a small thing. But, in crafting narratives about Black Americans, explaining how they are important, and claiming why we should study history in this way, our students are actually doing quite a big thing. They are not only speaking up to their teachers and classmates, but speaking outward at centuries of powerful individuals and institutions, including presidents like Jefferson and institutions like slavery, which have insisted on other narratives about Black Americans.

As I understood it in high school, my family's history—their immigration from different corners of Europe at the turn of the 20th century and integration into American life—was also part of a narrative that I inherited from older generations and bigger institutions. However, it was not one that I needed to challenge in order to make a claim for justice or dignify my place within the nation's history. I never felt the urgency or displayed the courage to revise the narrative around my own history that is on display in this book. For this reason, our students' work seems especially powerful to me. By writing, our students demonstrate that American history can be reexamined and revised, and that by sharing their voices they can have an influence on its future.

What I've learned from my students—and what I think all teachers in high schools and colleges should hear too—is that young scholars have much to say on this score. Many students are dissatisfied with classroom and popular narratives that reduce Black history to the anguish of slavery or the triumph of Civil Rights. Students seem to seek an understanding of our nation's history that is more complex, less comforting, and which has the potential to guide us better into the future. I feel confident that we have a rising generation of students ready to do this, which I find truly excellent.

Taneal Hogan

I believe black excellence should be taught in school, as it is important that we learn about it so that black folks themselves can deeply understand their worth as well as all others can understand too. I believe that it is also important to learn because black people don't receive as much credit for their work as they deserve. I think it is very important that we learn in school because in the outside world we won't really be taught about all the things we have accomplished. Other places you could possibly learn about it is in your home or black foundations. The way I would like to be taught about it in school is reading primary sources from people that represent black excellence or even actually being able to talk to them. I believe that black excellence shouldn't only be taught in certain classes such as history, but in all classes, It could be learned in classes like math or science by us talking about the first black mathematician or the first black scientist to win a Nobel Prize.

We have so many people that show black excellence, A great example is Dave Chappelle. He is a professional actor and comedian who started off young. As he got older and his career grew he started using his career to fight against racism. He had a show that mixed humor with racial scenarios and flipped the script, showing viewers how it would look if blacks were treated like the whites and the whites were treated like the blacks are treated. His career also gave him a voice so he spoke out on a lot of racial problems in the world, like when he spoke about the George Floyd killing. He is an example of black excellence because he didn't just sit around and do nothing and used his career and power as an advantage to speak up for all black people around the world. Also he can really inspire people because he started off young which can influence other people to start young on their dreams to be dedicated and hard working and don't let nothing stop or limit them.

Another person that really displays black excellence is Kevin Durant. He is a NBA player, one of the best that also started off young. He won MVP and also was a all-american im both high school and college. He uses his career and big image to fight against racism because he speaks out about the problems that happen in the world against black folks. Also he uses his platform and the fact that a lot of people know the NBA as an opportunity to give back. Him and other players have programs to give back to the communities that are less fortunate, And have partnerships to help out with giving back.He is an example of black excellence because he used the advantages he had for a positive thing, helping people out when they really needed it, And sharing his words on behalf of the black community. He also is a great example because he succeeded at his dream being a hard working, motivated person not letting nothing stop him, so he succeeded and excelled his dream.

A person that showed black excellence that we don't get to learn about in school, Tupac Shakur. Tupac should be learned about in school and it really is important that we learn about him because even though he is gone, his music and everything still has a huge impact on what is going on today in the US. He protested through his music. Not only did he talk about the problems blacks had with whites, He talked about the problem black had with blacks he told both sides about what they needed to fix. He told us blacks that if we want to solve the war about equality and peace we have to solve the black on black war in the streets because we won't be able to win the equality war if we can't even stand together as a united front. Also he shed light on a whole lot of other problems happening everyday that everyone else seems to just pass by as if it is not a problem. He is an example of black excellence because he spoke up and spoke his mind no matter who it was. He is still relevant to this day.

In conclusion, school and life overall will change if we celebrate black excellence because then people would see how great the black community is. To me black excellence means any type of success, and just making some type of positive impact even if it's just on a couple of people. Dave Chappelle, Kevin Durant, And Tupac Shakur are great examples of black excellence, And they show it everyday. I will show my black excellence by first doing what i have to to succeed so that when i have what i need to give back to my community, I can give it to them. I will also show black excellence by doing what I can as soon as I can to get the black community To stand together instead of fighting each other. But for now I will succeed at whatever I can right now to keep the people around me proud and do the right thing. Also by setting a good example for the younger people around me.

Stephanie Griffin

The definition of black excellence to me is that everyone should have the right to know about the past. This includes things like slavery, and we should know that historicial men and women fought to learn how to read and write and make a big change to achieve something more. We should all have a chance to know the excellence of being black in such a racist society so we can spread the love and let everyone know that they have to do better for a change.

The way many citizens of different races can show the support of blm/black excellence is by going to a rally to be heard. But we should not use too much power but just the right amount to make sure no one is getting killed. During BLM protests everyone is surrounded by police and black protestors to jail, but when the whites stormed the Capitol and broke the glass in the senate building nobody got arrested. This difference is important and shows why we need to appreciate black excellence more.

They would benefit by learning about what the blacks have gone through, why we go through the things been through. Our ancestors were beaten and brutally raped to the point where they could not walk or speak. This history that our ancestors experienced they would have wanted us to acknowledge in the back of our minds so we can have better understanding when we go out there and protest. we know what were protests getting locked up masted and beaten in the criminal system having to be recording because a rude white woman thinks we stole something and showing that we can be smart like our ancestors and we can have a march Martin Luther King once said I have and the black lawyers fighting for justice, doctors, some even have black owned business or companies where they hire blacks tangled up in the injustice which is set up so that blacks get a higher sentence than the white men and women that did the same crime get less time.

Mr. Carter G Woodson wanted to set an example to the young black Americans that you can make it out of any hard position and that's always a better way out so they go to college and learn about the things of his ancestors. He wanted black boys and girls to go out into the community and protest and to become important and have a part in changing racism in society for the betterment of the world. He made his influence by writing very scholarly books and magazine articles. Mr. Woodson was reaching out the negro schools to his books there schools so that young black boys and girls can know right from wrong and learn how to stand up for their rights in a way without breaking the law or any laws at all or at the time.

The Black Excellence Project
Sakiyah Hicks

The definition of Black Excellence to me is a black woman or man reaching their goals in life and making a name for themselves and doing what they believe is right. It is important to learn about black excellence especially for black people so they can know that people who came from their background made a difference in the world. It can also push us more to make a difference. I also believe that it is important to learn about black excellence in school because some kids don't learn about it at home and I think everybody should learn about it and not just people of color. Personally other than at school I learn black excellence at home and watch movies about black history. I think black excellence should be taught in every class because there have been many black women who loved science and math and wanted to do things with it but we are told they couldn't because they were females or black.

A lot of people have shown black excellence such as Martin Luther King Jr., Maya Angelou, Rosa Parks, Harriet Tubman, and others. We all have learned about them at school or at home and we learn about these same people over and over because they all have left a mark on this world for people of color. They represent us and what we stand for. They have changed the world in their own way through many social justice revolutions across the world such as the " Martin Luther King Day Parade" when we march in his honor so people won't forget what he sacrificed for us to even be able to do the things that we do today. These people are an example of black excellence because they stood up for what they believed in and thought was right even in the harsh world they were living in at the time. Many others and I respect that, especially when you felt or experienced what they went through.

Another person I would want to learn about is Regina Hall because I never really learned anything about her or what she does to be for black excellence. We learn about the same people all the time. I think it's time to learn about new people and what they did or do for black excellence because what I realized by typing this that I don't really know a lot of people of black excellence then the same ones we learn in school. It matters to learn about new people so we can know there are still people out there that care about our rights. I don't know a lot about Regina Hall but I know that she represents not only black excellence but also black women and I say this because black women or women period was always told they couldn't do this and that. Men always made a title for women because we weren't strong or smart enough to do the job.

I show my support of Black Excellence by believing in myself and others that we all can be something in life and leave our own mark on the world. I want people to talk about me every year and tell stories about how I changed the world.

B.E.P. Essay
Omari Holt

"Black Excellence: Someone who is black and portrays great qualities and abilities that make the black community proud." A quote directly from the urban dictionary. To me Black Excellence has a bit of a different meaning. Black is defined by the melanin in one's skin but not all black people have melanin. So to me Black Excellence is someone who is a part of the black community who succeeds and triumphs through life. You do not need to be rich or famous to be an example of black excellence. Due to this it goes overlooked a lot by the media and population which is why it is only right to teach it to kids. They should know about the success and hardships the people of their community went through so they don't grow up thinking that life will be easy. Often children are growing up facing these ideals that you must be popular or famous to be successful, you must look a certain way, or act a certain way which leads to disappointment. So by teaching kids Black Excellence not only in school but at home and around the community, it opens their brain to better possibilities for the future.

Black Excellence isn't a subject that should be specifically taught a certain way or in a certain class. People of the Black Community have made a breakthrough on many different topics in society. So I believe the topic of Black Excellence should be taught in all subjects. Math and Science celebrate the accomplishments of mathematicians and scientists, so why not teach about black mathematicians and scientists. Instead of always teaching about Albert Einstein or Newton let's take a break and learn about Benjamin Banneker or Kelly Miller. Black Excellence shouldn't be a topic that is only taught in specific classes because the black community contributes to all subjects.

By this time in society everyone should know of the famous Martin Luther King. He along with other famous black activists such as Malcolm X, Rosa Parks, Mary Church Terrell and many others are always taught about in school. They were all educated people of the black community despite all the educational barriers placed in their way to prevent them from being successful. Each of them were activists who caught for the black community in their own way but all with the same goal of Equal Rights. If we think life is unfair for the black community now while we protest and march through the streets we inhabit, these people had rules during their time that wouldn't even allow them to do half the stuff we do. They fought during times where open racism wasn't even looked over; it was celebrated. That's why they are examples of Black Excellence because throughout all their lives barriers separated them from success but even then they triumphed over all to reach their goals.

Many people in our modernized world show their support for the Black Community and our hardships. Black Lives Matter is our most popular organization that fights for equal rights. They tackle the fight for rights for not just Black people but for everyone within our community. I believe the organization should be researched more because people believe they are helping specifically colored people or specifically males. In reality Black Lives Matter is an organization that doesn't discriminate and all they wish for is for our lives to be taken into account also. They are an example of Black Excellence because they fight for the black community strong even when they are looked down upon by so many people. They are working to improve the community despite how many people stand against them or criticize them.

Black Excellence is a beautiful topic to learn about no matter where, when, how, or who you learn it from. Learning about a culture that is continuously trying to be covered is a way to ensure and help the black community. Having knowledge of us is already a step up from the ignorant people who ignore and criticize us. I am for black excellence and I show my support by continuing to do my best so I can grow and be like one of those famous activists I mentioned earlier. Someone who goes down in history not for the accomplishments they did for science, math or literature but instead for being known as someone who supported her community up until her dying breath. I wish Black Excellence was talked about more so maybe society wouldn't be so racist and acknowledge that the black community contributed to this world, too.

"The Black Excellence Project"
Jaelyn Watts

Black excellence reflects someone who is African-American and depicts great characteristics and abilities that make the African-American community proud. Black excellence, a state of being, produced from "Limitless, boundless, selfless." I think it's important for us to learn black excellence in school because everybody needs to know that the sky's the limit for us. Other places to learn about black excellence is on social media, or trending articles online. Black excellence can be placed into any subject honestly because there are black people that exceed at everything like math, art, science, etc. School and life could change by us celebrating black excellence simply by bringing everyone in the community together. I feel like by celebrating black excellence the African American community could become closer and possibly less violent if we just support each other.

Michelle Obama is somebody I think about when I hear black excellence. She was the first African-American first lady, and she also used to be an attorney. She worked in non-profits and as the associate dean of Student Services at the University of Chicago. While she was first lady, Michelle Obama was an advocate for poverty awareness and more. Michelle Obama was really all about wellness and health. In 2010, she started "Let's Move!" which was to bring everyone together and shed light on childhood obesity. She used her career to educate people on racism and try to bring everyone together. She represents black excellence in all ways to me.

I show my support for black excellence by working for a black-owned business and volunteering for a black-owned company. I also support by going to local pop up shops that have all black-owned businesses and purchase things. Also, I support all my friend's black businesses whether it's sharing their websites, instagram posts, or buying something and advertising it. It is important for me and my community to support our peers black businesses, even people we don't know. It is important to do this to show them that we care and that we respect their hustle and work ethic. It's completely free to support black businesses, a simple share will go a long way.

In conclusion, Black excellence is within all of us African Americans. You just have to find the right motivation to bring it out of you. Now is the time to show the world what you can do. Especially with covid-19 and quarantine going on people are bound to support a business or any endeavour that you come up with. No procrastination, no saying "I can't" because you can. You can do anything that you set your mind to. Even if somebody is already doing something that you're thinking about doing, it doesn't matter, just do it better.

Black Excellence Project
Michai Moore

My definition of Black Excellence is a Black person who refuses to give into the stereotypes of black people like being lazy, or looking for attention the wrong way. Instead, it's someone who achieves their goals, who doesn't give up and is going to stand up against injustice for anyone. Someone of any race can be for Black Excellence by being there and just being supportive. In other words, everyone can show support for Black Excellence by being there and cheering them on. Someone from any race would benefit from learning Black Excellence by not focusing on the bad because the majority of black people show Black Excellence everyday, it just doesn't go viral or is broadcasted on the news and on social media.

What Black Excellence means to me is when a black person is successful despite all of the obstacles against them, standing strong and pushing through. It is important to learn about Black Excellence because learning about someone who looks like me and learning that they didn't settle for less or take the easy way out is inspiring and it gives me hope. I do believe it is important to learn in schools because some people don't have the chance of learning about Black Excellence other than at school. I learn about Black excellence from my mom and sometimes social media. Black excellence should be taught in all subjects. What I would expect in math and science to celebrate Black Excellence is by acknowledging the black people who have made their mark on math and science.

Anna Julia Cooper is an example of black excellence. Copper was born into salvery, became a well known author, activist, and educator. Her most important work is *A Voice from the South: By a Black Woman of the South.* Her professional and educational pathway is Augustine's Normal School and Collegiate which was a school for freed slaves. While she was still in school she started teaching math, then she noticed that her male classmates were studying a more rigorous curriculum than the females, and after that she started advocating for the education of black women. Cooper used her career to fight racism by enlightening people on how black women are treated. Anna Julia Cooper is an example of black excellence because instead of being silent she stood against racism and sexism against black women and wrote a book from her perspective as a black woman showing how she and other black women felt. She also condemned some people who weren't there for black women.

I would want to learn more about Dave Chapelle. It matters to learn about this individual because it is important to know that there can be Black Excellence in things other than doctors lawyers and other professions. Using your platform to make people happy and to also speak on important issues is Black Excellence. Dave Chappelle is another example of Black Excellence by him being able to speak on a lot or controversial topics in a way that people can laugh at but still understand. Another way he is an example of Black Excellence is that he is not afraid to say how he feels and he doesn't sugarcoat anything.

I am for Black Excellence, I think that the more people learn about it the more it can inspire black people to do great things. I will show my support for black excellence by showing Black Excellence in my life. Black excellence is an amazing way to celebrate black people. However, I think my only concern is that it almost always focuses on Michelle Obama or Dr. Martin Luther King Jr. and other famous figures. Which isn't a bad thing, it's just that there are more modern people that show black excellence, like Taraji P Henson or Dave Chappelle who are a lot more relatable. In conclusion I am for Black Excellence and as much as I love to learn about the people before me who show Black Excellence, I would like to relate to some people and I think we should talk about more modern people when it comes to Black Excellence.

Mekayla Gulley
12/16/20
History of the Americas

Black Excellence Project

Black Excellence is the African American's showcasing and staging their beliefs and abilities. This makes the black community proud by showing their abilities. It helps the black community not only with motivation but with multiple benefits. Other races can support Black excellence by showcasing the abilities, talents, and other accomplishments. of the black community. They can also believe in black excellence and support people in the black community positively. I think people should learn about black excellence because everyone deserves to get credit for what they do like other public figures. Other races can benefit from black excellence by being seen as a person who supports others and uses their talents and abilities for good use. This means that you are willing to help other people, especially people who are going through a lot, for instance by being supportive, helpful, and reliable. Therefore, every school should learn about black excellence as well as in museums, conventions, and other venues.

It is important to learn about black excellence because it helps inform people who need to appreciate black culture. In my interview I selected a person who fit that role. I would say that her job is important because her job requires her to contribute to the education of people around the world. Also, she is a project manager that presents good ideas to her team that benefits a lot of people. Her job combats racism by her constantly bringing different communities together and making them one. Next, she exemplifies black excellence by being quite productive in the community as a black woman.

She also happens to remind me of a leader in the black community: Michelle Obama. Despite the amount of the things they have done for people she reminds me of Michelle because of her attributes. Therefore, they are similar because of their positivity, leadership, and encouragement. Michelle Obama has helped a lot of people and has constantly worked to put others first. She is a pillar in the community and makes black women proud. She also tells me that no matter where you are in life you can do important things.

I happen to encourage black excellence so much because I aspire to show black excellence one day. I would use my generosity to help build institutions and foundations. Black excellence is important because black people did so much for this country and deserve more recognition. Also, I believe it can inspire other poc (people of color) to be entrepreneurs. Black excellence isn't just about accreditation it is also about encouragement. Next, the people who represent black excellence also have helped people academically as well.

My school life would change by school being more productive if we celebrated black excellence. I believe this to be true because we would have a lot of activities for black excellence. Since, I go to a predominately black school it would be very influential. In conclusion, it would help influence students and maybe give them a chance to show their talents and abilities.

London Haynie

Black Excellence is an important and complex mindset which is followed by constant acts of bravery by Black people. Black Excellence means to rise up above the struggles of racism and become a great success or impact on our communities and others. Black Excellence is a significant topic to be educated on because learning about the struggles and victories of Black people will help everyone to be better understood. Understanding of Black people and their history is necessary because mutual understanding and appreciation brings less conflict and more love to all diverse communities. It is also important to learn about in school because students learn about all of the achievements of America without highlighting every group of people who greatly contributed to the creation of the United States. Black Excellence should be taught in every school subject by shining a light on various Black artists, scientists, mathematicians, and even more, because these people are underrepresented in most fields that they thrive in.

A valuable exemplar of Black Excellence could be a famous Black person, or any Black person we may come across. A great friend of mine, Peyton Holmes, is an example of someone who I consider as Black Excellence. Peyton Holmes is a student who attends Woodrow Wilson High School in Washington, D.C. and is currently in the ninth grade. She was born in Atlanta, Georgia, but has lived in the District of Columbia for almost her whole life. When I took the opportunity to interview her, I gained a unique insight on Black Excellence, which may be very different from other people's views on the matter. Coming from someone who is around my age, I expected to receive answers that would be polar opposite to a response from an accomplished and successful adult. Peyton Holmes proved me right. Her distinct view on the term Black Excellence was compelling. Peyton views it as a simple way of living life as a Black person, requiring no effort to be particularly excellent. But, simply surviving in a world that is against you, "freely and happily," she states. Peyton Holmes is truly an example of Black Excellence purely because she is a young Black woman living in a society that does not want the best for her and is working against, instead of for people like her. Black people who strive everyday to defeat the odds of racism and oppression are all embodiments of the term Black Excellence.

Black mathematicians are also examples of Black Excellence. Mathematics has been viewed as a White subject since the beginning of civilization. Math is said to have come from the Greeks and Europeans. Taking this into consideration, it must be hard for Black mathematicians to get the representation that they deserve. Black people are usually seen as unintelligent and incapable compared to their White peers. Although these false stereotypes have been forced into today's culture, Black mathematicians still continue to persevere and work through it which makes them great examples of Black Excellence. One specific example of a Black mathematician is Euphemia Lofton Haynes. In 1943, Lofton Haynes was the first Black woman to earn a Ph.D. in math. This is a very significant accomplishment because racism against Black people was very popular during this time. It is important to learn about mathematicians of color because they are extremely underrepresented in the math field. Black mathematicians need support and representation so that there can continue to be role models for Black kids who love math.

Anyone, of any race, can support Black Excellence. To support Black Excellence means to celebrate, connect, invest time in, and be an ally to the Black community and all of the individual people within it. Someone who is not Black can benefit from learning about Black Excellence because it will show them who is the backbone of this nation they are a part of. Learning about this will bring everyone the education it takes to respect and love Black people. I personally feel that I am a part of Black Excellence. I am also in support of all of the excellent Black people. I show my support of Black Excellence by sharing Black people's successes, and uplifting Black people when they are in need of support.

Finally, it may be concluded that Black Excellence is an important mindset, action, and movement. Celebrating Black Excellence would make a difference to the whole world because it would decrease, and hopefully end, the racism and prejudice against Black people. It would bring more groups of people together and lessen the hate and negativity that we have all across the world. All Black people can represent Black Excellence and all people can be for Black Excellence. From the words of Oprah Winfrey, another outstanding representation of Black Excellence, "I was raised to believe that excellence is the best deterrent to racism or sexism. And that's how I operate my life." I believe that all Black people can operate their life in the ways of excellence, and am hopeful that this will in fact deter racism in order to build a better society for generations to come.

Lashawna Liverpool

It is important to learn about Black excellence because it's important to know about our culture and community. In the area you live in you can learn about Black excellence. In school I want to learn about Black excellence as a team and we take important notes about it. No, it shouldn't be taught in just certain subjects; it should be known everywhere. To celebrate Black excellence in math and science I would expect a happy gathering community.

The most significant aspect about Ashley's professional's background is her being a teen mom and taking care of her child on her own with no guidance. Ashley is my cousin who was a young parent. Ashley's personal pathway is to make sure she and her child are successful in life. Ashley uses her career to fight racism to stay strong and not give up. She is an example of Black excellence because she isn't giving up. Ashley's history is to continue her life and be successful. Her professional background is her, having a child at a young age and as she grows and grows, does what she can best to take care of her child on her own. The Important moments in Ashley's life is that she never gave up. The challenges she faced was being a teen mom. Ashley is an example of Black Excellence because she stayed strong no matter how much she was struggling. I feel like Ashley is a good and responsible person.

It is important to learn about President Obama because at one point he was a leader to the whole world and others looked up to him. Obama is an example of Black excellence because people look at him as an example to our community. Obama was the first African American president of the United States. Obama was a prolific politician and was revered by the American public especially from his home state of Illinois and city of Chicago.

Someone of any race can be for Black Excellence if they support Black Excellence. People can show support for Black Excellence by showing positivity to others. Someone from any race benefiting from learning about Black Excellence is getting to know about it and asking questions but it's all about supporting each other.

I will show my support of Black excellence by helping others out in my community if I see that someone needs help. My life will overall change if we celebrate Black excellence because some people are racist people like to go against each other and other negative things. Black excellence is very important to people like me and our world. WE ALL NEED TO WORK TOGETHER AS A TEAM.

Black Excellence Project
La'Nyia Rogers

My definition of black excellence is when someone can positively impact society or the world which will result in the future and they'll most likely be remembered. Someone from any race can be for black excellence by just supporting a movement that someone has made and help with the movement so there can be a solution to the problem. Someone from any race can benefit from learning black excellence because they could realize certain things about themselves and change them by just reading up on black excellence. Most of the people that are shown in the category of black excellence fought for their rights or just something that possibly changed the world.

The person I chose to interview was no one other than my mother (who actually helped me finish the assignment). For the first question I wanted to know what she thought Black Excellence was and she replied "Black Excellence is when an African American takes a stand against something they know is wrong." As a thought I said "well I actually agree" because although it was a common answer there was no right or wrong answer. "One person that represented black Excellence is Harriet Tubman," she said and I agreed with her and her response because if you know what Black Excellence is I'm pretty sure the first person anyone will name Harriet Tubman because she is one of the bravest and most intelligent leaders that lived. "One way I can represent Black Excellence is by leading the community," she said. Her response tells me how she is willing to help the community. And lastly the final two answers. For the first one she replied "I would support a movement for equality" which I thought was a great answer because of present events and for the second one she said "I represented Black

Excellence by voting and made a big impact by doing so." And this response actually was a little surprising because my mother has an injury and she can't work or do a lot of stuff, so when she said her vote made an impact, I couldn't do anything but agree.

Another example for Black Excellence is Frederick Douglass. I believe it's important to learn about Frederick Douglass because when you think about it he made a big difference. Douglass actually was a kid who wanted to learn to read and write. In case you didn't know, he was a slave and slaves weren't allowed to know how to read and write because the whites that owned slaves and plantations wanted the blacks to be dumb and not have the power that reading and writing provides. But Douglass didn't give up and wanted education and knowledge that most slaves couldn't receive. Douglass also had help from his master's children and as a slave that was brave to try something so risky. In addition to that Douglass actually became an educator/author and made it possible for black children to learn how to read and write.

I, La'Nyia Rogers, am for Black Excellence. The way I support Black Excellence is by learning everything past leaders did to make an impact in my future and act on it because at a point in time the world was super unfair and now we can use the same bathrooms and slavery is abolished. And I can honestly be able to make a difference for the future as well if I just try and believe in myself because most of the past black leaders of the world actually struggled to make something happen but they just continued to try and not give up or lose hope.

In conclusion, I think if we celebrated Black Excellence as a holiday or event school and life would be different because although there is a black history month we still don't learn everything about that black history. And by different I mean learning further than any school has before because there is more history than we've learned in all the years we were in school.

Black Excellence SteSenia Gibson
Ste'jonn Gibson

What is Black Excellence to me? It is knowing your worth instead of going by what other races believe. It is coming on top as the underdog. It is believing you can do it. They are who inspire her life and motivates her to keep going strong and never to give up. Schools need to teach more about black excellence instead of the same three people we learn about every year. I think a good way to promote black excellence is to have every subject talk about an African American who has accomplished something great within that subject. Another place to learn about black excellence, believe it or not, is social media.

I did my Black Excellence interview on SteSenia VerKisha Gibson. She's a 33 year old single mother of a boy. She stated she gets her motivation from her son, mom and sister. I've decided to interview Ms. SteSenia and here are the responses. I started by explaining what the interview was about as well as asking for her permission to record her responses. "Do you mind sharing your age and a little history about yourself? Like are you a parent, married?" I asked. She responded with, "Sure! I'm 33 years old, I have 1 son who I love and wouldn't trade him for the world, except for the days he makes me mad, haha! And no, I'm not married." I continued with asking, "Who inspires you? What are your goals?" She seemed proud to answer this. "My mother. She never looked down at me, especially when I became a teen mom at 19. Just to see my mom smile at all my accomplishments is what motivates me and inspires me to grind harder. Also, my son. Just when he says he's proud of me and one day I'm going to make us rich motivates me. One of my goals is to finish school by the Summer of 2021 and graduate. I'm working towards my BA at UDC. Then, I would love to land a job at an Elementary or Middle School. My last goal is to buy a whole neighborhood to house my mom, dad, sister, brother and their children and, of course, my son." Now that I've gotten to know her a bit more, I decided to move on to the next topic. I jumped straight into the questions. "What do you think shows black Excellence?" SteSenia replied with, "I think being a part of the black community and giving back shows black Excellence. Being that voice. Speaking up. Taking actions. Being an advocate."

I think some good examples of black excellence are the wonderful women who founded the Black Lives Matter movement: Alicia Garza, Patrisse Cullors, and Opal Tometi. It is very important to learn about this movement, not only to educate yourself but to be able to educate others. They encourage equality in our world and they do it peacefully. They have done many protests, speeches and more to promote us as people. Their movement is not to belittle other races, saying their race does not matter, but to improve equality and love for African Americans, which is why they are a great example of black excellence.

I would like to think that I am for black excellence. I believe we are all meant to be equal, we are all beautiful, and we should stand as one. I will prove to younger black boys and girls that the color of your skin should not determine who you have to be just because of society's thoughts. We are powerful, beautiful and intelligent. We have to prove not to the others but to ourselves that we are worthy and able.

To conclude, since we spend more time dealing with school than anything else, we should have more opportunities to learn about black excellence. We should not only learn about the same three people. We should not only learn about black excellence in February. We should learn about black excellence at least once a week, a highlight of some sorts. Children, especially, need this because they need to know how worthy they are. Black is beautiful, black is amazing, black is excellence.

Black Excellence
Justus Williams

My definition of Black Excellence isn't a concept that belongs to singular individuals who are being excellent. I see Black Excellence as a successful community of Black people all being excellent. Everyone can show Black Excellence by supporting Black people and Black culture. I think Black excellence should be taught everywhere. The real question is if the lesson will resonate with students if we learn about it in school. If we can learn about Black Excellence in school it should be taught wherever it was applied because Black people have many accomplishments in a variety of different fields.

A great example of an Excellent Black Man is Jason Reynolds. Reynolds is an African-American author who writes novels and poetry for young adult and middle-grade audiences. He has earned many nominations and awards for his books, including a Newbery Medal in 2018 for his book called the "Long Way Down" (which is a great book to read). Reynolds's philosophy is that he doesn't like to read or write uninteresting books, which may be why he started writing books. Reynolds wants to write non-boring books that are entertaining, educational, and also relatable in order to dispute the theory of books being boring. Jason Reynolds is a great example of Black Excellence because he is helping so many young black men and boys in Ward 8 become interested in books because when it comes to literature in school most boys hate books because they find them dull. I like that Jason Reynolds does this because he is also trying to help his community become excellent by educating them with books, sort of like Frederick Douglass.

Another great example of an Excellent Black person is one of my former teachers and author Crystal M. Adair. Ms. Adair is a great example of an excellent Black Woman because of how amazing she is. Ms. Crystal is one of the most selfless, inspiring, and loving people you will ever meet. Her philosophy on black excellence is someone who "dares to live boldly and proudly in **this** skin every, single day and still persevere and achieve 'in spite of.'" And that is exactly what she does every day. Some of the biggest challenges she had to overcome were years of grief and depression following a series of traumatic events: namely, the sudden and back-to-back losses of her parents as a teenager, the subsequent verbal and physical abuse from a court-appointed guardian, and domestic violence at the hands of a sibling. In spite of all that adversity, Crystal M. Adair strived to achieve, turning her "test into a testimony by the grace of God". She went on to graduate from Clark Atlanta University with a degree in Mass Media Arts (Radio-Television-Film), write two inspirational books, and became an English Language Arts and Public Speaking instructor who dabbles in theater with a successful career of 21 years and counting.

I am for Black Excellence not only because I am Black but because I want to see my people succeed in life, whether that be individually or collectively. My way to support Black Excellence is to better myself so that I can attain the ability to empower myself and others in my community to achieve greater. I want to strive to do this through education. Knowledge is power and you never know who, what, when, or where you can learn something new. The sharing of wisdom is key to success because nobody can do something completely by themselves; they had to get the information needed from somewhere. That is why I am for strong Black people and communities sharing and gaining together.

Lastly, I think Black Excellence is recognized but is not really celebrated. In school. It's starting to become a little more glorified, but the concept hasn't fully received the respect it deserves. I say this because if we really celebrated Black Excellence African-Americans would feel much more appreciative and proud of the accomplishments our ancestors have made, not only in today's world but also in the past. This would lead us to try and take more active roles in many different parts of our present day society. For example, higher education in places like colleges. How many Black professors have you had? Another example is politics, even though we are getting more involved in that aspect of life, but how many Black senators have you seen? If Black people and Excellence were congratulated and accepted I think Black people would try to take more leadership roles in society.

Black Excellence
Anari Walters

My definition of black excellence is someone who does something that makes the black community proud. People can show support to black excellence by just doing little things like posting in support of others on Instagram, writing an article about them, and helping them with little things they need. Young people can benefit from learning about black excellence by seeing how someone came from being poor to now making their second book. This can give them the motivation that they can do it too. I do believe it's important to learn in school because not a lot of people know about this history. I think our parents should also teach us because we should know where we could be instead of knowing where we come from.

Ms. Tracey Eley is an outstanding example of black excellence as a police officer who faced many challenges in her life. In the interview I asked what was the most important success in her job, and she said "the most important was me becoming the first black female to make lieutenant on my job." I believe she represents black excellence because she is a role model to her friends and family and also people she comes in contact with. I asked how she overcame challenges that came across her way. She explained "by praying and staying focused". I also asked what she sees herself doing to help the community. She said "I used to work with young girls to teach them about being positive on the spiritual side". She is a good representation of black excellence in everything she does.

Another person who I think shows black excellence in many different ways is Harriet Tubman. Harriet escaped to freedom in 1849. She became the most famous conductor of the Underground Railroad. Harriet also helped the Union

Army during the Civil War. This shows many reasons for how she is black excellence. She helped more than 300 enslaved people in 19 trips. She helped many people throughout her lifetime. I look at her as black excellence because she did what people said she could not do because she was black and because she was female.

I think I show black Excellence in many ways. I think I show black excellence by being a role model for my peers. I show black excellence by being a role model to my family. I show support of black excellence by doing things like repost something or even liking it when it highlights black excellence in others. Also I support black excellence by sharing it with other people. And I will support black excellence in the future by teaching my kids and other people about it.

I think school would change a lot if we learned about black excellence because students would learn more about our culture and history. I think it will also change life because whites may look at blacks differently and this can also show blacks that they don't need to be ashamed of their skin color because their skin color means something. I think this will also help combat racism because this can also show whites that we are more than our skin color and our history.

On that note, I'd like to recap that Back Excellence is all over the world no matter where you are and we need more people for it.

-Angel Kinard

In my opinion, I do think people from other races should be given the opportunity to learn about Black Excellence because Black people weren't the only race to go through life changing things, other races have gone through life changing things and have been the cause of life changing things. Therefore, I think that people of other races should also learn about Black Excellence because their ancestors could have been doing things to harm Black people back then or their ancestors could have been trying to help Black people and they should be able to learn about it.

-Colby Drake

Angel Kinard

Black Excellence is a description of someone who has had their hardships and overcome them. An example is all of the overworked black parents who have multiple jobs just to survive. Or the black student in a mostly white school having their intelligence tested everyday by their classmates and teachers. Or even the homeless woman who asks for change wherever she goes. But sometimes it could be someone famous. Taraji P Henson is from the DMV like the majority of the kids in this school and not only did she make it out of here, she made it big. And that isn't at all easy and seeing as she did it anyway shows how she is an example of Black Excellence. Knowing that Black Excellence is how you describe a hard working African American is something that not many people know. Not too many schools actually teach the good parts of Black history, just only about slavery, so some people think that just becoming famous makes Black Excellence when really it's about how you get there and how much work you put in for it.

Ari Lennox is a singer who can be considered of Black Excellence since she worked hard to get where she is. She wasn't born into fame and she wasn't groomed to be a musician. She actually worked a lot of jobs in her early twenties. In an interview with GQ, Lennox speaks about how she started out singing covers on Youtube in her free time. Then the interviewer asks her if she had tried out on American Idol or something in that nature how she thinks she would have done and she straight up admits that in her early singing days of 2009 she would have embarrassed herself because she didn't know who she was at the time and she wasn't fully developed. I see this as her self reflection because she speaks on how at the start of her career, she wasn't ready compared to now and she worked hard on her music and on herself to get to this point. Her interview with GQ was amazing in my opinion because she really goes into detail about how much work she had to put into her music, herself, her environment and from what I read, that alone is why she represents Black Excellence.

Another example of Black Excellence, in my eyes, is my older brother, David. My brother is from DC as well and when he was young, maybe younger than me, he talked about how he wanted to grow up and live in New York to work. But David was never really a behind-the-desk worker, he's always been more into photography and getting out of the DMV is hard enough for people of color if it isn't a sit down job sometimes. But he put in enough work and tried his hardest, and currently he is doing photography and also modeling for other photographers while he is living in Manhattan, NY. He is literally getting paid to be creative and I can tell he's doing well with his work too since he always sends me pictures and links of articles either about him or with his interviews in them. He even made it onto Vogue magazine more than once and that is a pretty big accomplishment when trying to become famous the way he is. David is an example of Black Excellence because he made his childhood dream come true by putting in the work to get there and be at his level of fame.

There are many examples of Black Excellence all over the world as a matter of fact, but not even half of them are supported or backed up by other people unless they are an actor or someone famous. There are lots of celebrities who are supported and loved but hated on ten fold. Sometimes it's a racial thing, other times it's a jealousy thing, but no matter what it is there will always be the supporters and in the end that's what matters the most. Being against Black Excellence is mainly just not wanting to see any people of color succeed in life no matter how hard they work and there is no reason for wanting someone to fail at life. I will always be for Black Excellence because I am a person of color who would like to be supported in her dreams and because there are already so many people against or unsupportive of Black Excellence that we need everyone we can get.

Seeing as the supporters of Black Excellence are limited, schools should definitely teach the students about Black Excellence, especially the younger students. I say this because many children get raised in homes that don't support Black Excellence for whatever reason which will have them grow up the same way and continue the cycle. But if schools could get to the kids before their opinions and ideas are completely affected as a whole for the rest of their lives, they could stop the hatred being planted in the young generation's minds. Stopping the problem at its root not only is good for the children but it's good for the future. It'd be like a domino effect; the kids learn about Black Excellence then they teach it to their children who pass it on to their children and so on. The outcome of this would make life way more positive when it comes to race and supporting one another which would make life easier and a lot better for the next generation. On that note, I'd like to recap that Back Excellence is all over the world no matter where you are and we need more people for it.

We Are Black Excellence
Alaunee Pitts

Black Excellence is when a Black/African American does great things for the world and their community. When a person is showing black excellence they are making the black community proud. It's important to learn about Black Excellence because it can be very encouraging towards the black community and motivate us to do great things as well. I believe it is important to learn about black excellence in schools. It isn't just good for us to learn, it's also good for other races to learn more about our culture. It also can motivate other races and inform people that we are not negative people. Black Excellence can be taught in all subjects. There are black people that have achieved great things in all subjects such as math, English, science, and others. In math class we can talk about the black people who accomplished great things in math or created something in math that we use today.

An example of Black Excellence is my grandmother Maria Pearson. Maria was pregnant at a young age and lived in a difficult childhood but she was always bright. While in high school she worked and saved money so she will have the money to move into her own place. Maria lived with her mother and her sisters, but her older sister didn't really help much around the house so Maria had to help her mom a lot even though she had so many more responsibilities. Living in her house was very toxic so when she saved up her money nobody knew that she had the money. Maria was tired of all the trouble going on in her house so she finally moved into an apartment but it was still in the area so she could be familiar with everything. Her mom still didn't know what she was up to. She always assumed Maria was at her boyfriend's house. Saving money really helped her. Maria was a manager at Mcdonald's for 3 years, and now she works as a certified marketing consultant in a rental office and she's been in that business for 26 years. That is something Maria always wanted to be in life. She used her career to fight racism because she has gone through so much in her life and for her to accomplish her dreams and persevere she is proving society wrong. Maria is an example of Black Excellence because all her hard work and the kindness she spreads persuades her family to be great.

Zendaya Coleman is another example of Black Excellence. Zendaya is multi-talented and an amazing example for young black women who want to be something at a young age. Zendaya is an actress and a singer. "Zendaya started acting as a child, appearing in productions at the California Shakespeare Theater and other theatrical companies near her hometown of Oakland, California." (https://www.biography.com/actor/zendaya). She really came to fame in 2010 on her first television gig "Shake it Up" on Disney Channel. She also released her self-titled debut album in 2013. She starred in another disney series called "K.C. Undercover". She played in the movies Spider-man Homecoming (2017), Spider-Man: Far From Home (2019) , and The Greatest Showman(2017). She now plays the starring role Rue in the HBO series Euphoria which is different from the Disney image. Zendaya won an Emmy award for Lead actress in the drama series Euphoria. Zendaya is an example of Black Excellence because she has accomplished many things at a young age and it amazes me because I've been looking up to her since she's been on Disney Channel. Zendaya is always kindhearted and is a positive role model to the community.

I show Black Excellence by persevering to do a lot of great things at a young age and being able to have a mindset of an adult. Many adults talk bad about this generation but I like to prove them wrong. They feel as though we are not as intelligent and can't do the things they did as a child. I'm a very independent person. I like to get things done on my own. I enrolled myself in Bard by myself, I work, have my own money, and I'm trying to learn how to save so I can move out at 18. For me to go through a lot and do the things I do, lots of my friends are encouraged by my actions and that makes me happy because I want them to be great and succeed as well. I show my support to Black Excellence by believing in myself and my community. We might not do good things all the time but when we work together and do great stuff for our community we are powerful.

If Black Excellence was celebrated in school and overall in the world our community will be so powerful. So many people would be encouraged by us and not see us as how society looks at us currently. There are so many of us that have benefited from this world in so many ways but are so underrated. If Black Excellence was taught in school it would be taught in every subject because there are black people that have done great things in math, English, science, art, music, etc. Overall in the world if black excellence was celebrated people would see how brilliant we are and not just recognize the bad things about our community everyday from what they see on social media or how we were explained back in the day. It would be better if they got to hear our story officially and understand how we feel and how we can be a positive influence to our world. If black excellence was celebrated we would be dominant and all people would be able to come together.

Anthony J. Green
12/15/20
History of Americas: Black Excellence Project

Generational Black Excellence

In my opinion, Black excellence means the embodiment of power, intelligence, inspiration, and greatness in the black community. Depictions of the accomplishments and success of Black people in the media is lackluster. In contrast with this under representation in the media, learning about black excellence is important in the school system because it could be used to inspire the youth of the black community. For example, say a young black girl learned about Naomi Osaka or Serena Williams in school. She would be inspired by the example these powerful black women have set. Imagine how many young aspiring actors, athletes, mathematicians, engineers, and architects we would have if we were taught more about them and their greatness. I believe that it is important that Black excellence is taught in school to inspire the youth and educate them on what they could one day be.

Learning about the accomplishments of black individuals in a range of professions can have a powerful influence on students and schools. For example Black excellence could be taught in mathematics by learning from the mathematicians of the black community. In literature Black excellence is taught by reading African American authors or authors of African descent. The same thing could be said about science, where one can learn about Black scientists.

I feel as though it's more important to learn about your culture and see more representatives of greatness in a community in which you're a part. I have learned about Black excellence online, in articles, social media, and by self education and research. I feel like Black excellence should be taught in history more often than being educated on racism and slavery which we've been accustom to for years. Constantly familiarized with the anguish our enslaved ancestors had to endure, this can be depressing for some. Especially when you see so much racial injustice being normalized in the media. On the contrary this year in history we've learned of great Black individuals throughout history: slaves who had escaped, African American abolitionists, and former slaves who wrote about their experiences.

Naomi Osaka is a great example of excellence in the black community, representing Black excellence with her profound tennis skills, her resolve to speak out and aid the Black community even with constant discrimination, and using her platform to speak on the injustices that have occurred in society recently. Born Oct 16, 1997, Naomi Osaka, a Japanese professional tennis player. ranked No. 1 by the Women's Tennis Association, and is the first Asian player to hold the top ranking in singles. She is a three-time Grand Slam singles champion, and is the reigning champion at the US Open. Osaka comes from an interracial household: her father Hatian, and mother Japanese. So she is considered to be "Blasian" (Black and Asian). Coming from Japan and having a darker complexion, she was often talked about as "too dark to be Japanese, but not black enough to be black" or "sunburnt," as said in an essential sports article. Being mixed should not make her any less black than the next person as her father is of Hatian/African descent. Even though she faces these hardships she still combats racism in the U.S. While competing in 2020 Osaka consistently used her platform to keep the Black Lives Matter movement and recent victims of police brutality. When she stepped onto the court for her first U.S. Open match this year, she surprised the world with a powerful tribute to Breonna Taylor, who was murdered by police while asleep in her home.

Another example of Black excellence is Katherine Johnson, who performed an extraordinary task that went down in history. Katherine Coleman Goble Johnson was an American mathematician who was a crucial part to the success of the first and subsequent U.S. crewed space flights, due to her calculations in orbital mechanics. Throughout history women have confronted an uphill battle. This consists of being racially oppressed, having less rights, and getting less representation in male-dominated fields, for example, S.T.E.M (Science, Technology, Engineering, and Mathematics). Although it seems that women haven't done anything in those "male-dominated fields," on the contrary they have done a lot. Most people know Neil Armstrong as the "first man on the moon" and this famous line, "one small step for man." This might not have happened without this woman. Just weeks after Katherine Johnson began a position as one of Langley Research Center's human computers in 1952. There, Johnson performed the NASA calculations that made possible the manned space missions of the early 1960s as well as the 1969 moon landing. In reference to this, the movie 'Hidden Figures' features another amazing Black woman, Taraji P. Henson, who plays Johnson. In the movie they portray the female scientists who were hired at NASA to be human computers, crunching numbers and solving complex equations while WWII commenced.

Am I for Black excellence? This question shouldn't have to be asked. I center all of my writings based on the challenges we face in the Black community in hopes of broadcasting the thoughts of a young black man. I try my best to use my writing to convey my opinions on the racial, criminal, and systemic injustices we face. I will continue to try to spread these opinions and highlight what goes on in this world. What I have done for Black excellence is submit one of my best writings into the Bard Highschool magazine. The writing is called 'The Diary of An Intelligent Black Teen.'

Another way I'd like to show Black excellence is by making a change. I strive to become a symbol for kids who are like me. Being an example of accomplishing great feats, even with the odds stacked against you.

In conclusion, I believe that if Black excellence were taught in school the kids of the future and present would aspire to be great like the people they look up to. There would be a never ending loop of greatness and inspiration. Great people inspiring the young to be great. Making an example for the next generation. In other words intergenerational inspiration. Along with this should be an increase of Black excellence being broadcasted in the media. It would be great to see more positivity in the Black community especially to the younger generations, rather than to see how there has been people mistreated.

Black Excellence Project
Colby Drake

To me, Black excellence is a person who is willing to put their life on the line to fight for what's right. This person holds a lot of power and they are very significant. Black excellence is a big topic and something you can learn a lot about and from. Black excellence is mainly shown through people, whether old or young, including both our ancestors and people now. I also think Black Excellence defies and magnifies slavery and everything else significant that happened to black people and what they have overcome.

I feel as though the topic Black Excellence and everything else that comes with it should be taught in schools, especially in history and reading classes. I feel they should be taught in those classes and school in general because kids deserve to know about what their ancestors went through and they should know what people back then had to go through just to get where they are now. If the students are comfortable enough they should be able to see what happened, how different things were back then, and how differently Black people were treated. They should be taught this also because the things that happened to people back then could have been them in that position. Lastly, I think kids should be taught this topic in school because they should be able to look at the situation and everything that happened and decipher who they think identifies Black Excellence. In my opinion, I do think people from other races should be given the opportunity to learn about Black Excellence because Black people weren't the only race to go through life changing things, other races have gone through life changing things and have been the cause of life changing things. Therefore, I think that people of other races should also learn about Black Excellence because their ancestors could have been doing things to harm Black people back then or their ancestors could have been trying to help Black people and they should be able to learn about it.

I feel as though there are many people who define Black Excellence. Some of the people I feel define Black Excellence are Rosa Parks, Thurgood Marshall, Malcolm X, and Dr. Martin Luther King, Jr. There are many more but these are a couple of examples. Those people and everyone else define Black Excellence for me because they all stood up for what was right for their culture and they all played a part in doing something to help us get to where we are today. There are also some people alive today who are trying to help the Black community and still try to continue the legacy of our ancestors.

Someone from my family I feel defines Black Excellence is my mother. She was born and grew up in Washington, D.C. She went to college for law and currently works as a manager in customer service. A couple of her successes are being a single mother, maintaining a career, and raising a productive member of society. As a result of quarantine, I have had the ability to see her coach and mentor her team members on a daily basis. She is a teaching boss. She is a supervisor and lead trainer for a federal government call center. In her role she manages a team of 17-25 call center agents and trainees, all new hires, and provides refreshers for the incumbent staff. She has raised children her whole life to include myself and her siblings.

I don't think school would change much for some people but for others it might impact school a lot meaning that if schools didn't already celebrate Black excellence by having a Black history program they might start to have them. Also, if schools celebrated Black Excellence students might be informed of how important this topic is to some people and the significance in Black Excellence. In life, I think it would change a lot because already we have some movements supporting black excellence or black history standing up for what's right. Overall, I think it would change a lot because people will not only stand up for what's right but also they will realize Black people's worth.

Sonie W.

Black excellence to me is when a colored person is achieving/heading their goal. They may have reached it, but mainly when an African American concurs their goal/dream. I see that she has dedication for what she wants in life.

For my black excellence project, I based it off my aunt Marchelle who really inspires me daily. I chose her for the black excellence project because of my definition of black excellence. I asked her a few questions to get a better understanding of what she really wants and how she relates to black excellence. Marchelle currently works as a crisis worker within the black community in Richmond, VA. She assists with stabilizing moods of people who deal with mental diagnosis. Her goal is to prevent her clients from hospitalization while giving them the support and good will they need in their community. She is also a hair stylist in her community. She uses her talents to strengthen the bond between culture and business. Her college journey inspired her. While she was in college, she experienced things that propelled her towards her goal. Those opportunities were something that broke generational patterns in her family. The gap between her community and her experiences inspired her to work towards providing for those in her community. A combination of her parents and supportive women in her family inspired her toward where she is today. From her younger ages, women around her taught her how to find a common ground between being nurturing yet assertive in her quest for excellence. Her definition of black excellence is when a colored person reaches their goal of success in a world of obstacles.

Another person for black excellence was Chadwick Boseman. Chadwick was an African American actor who played in multiple American films, such as Black Panther, Get

On Up, Marshall and many more. His first film was 42, the Jackie Robinson movie. He was born November 29, 1976 and passed on August 28, 2020. He graduated from Howard University in 2000, also with a bachelor of Fine Arts in directing. Black excellence to me is a big thing. It is about supporting or achieving goals.

I support black excellence by trying to support the people who are striving to do something, such as business, art, and in other fields. I like to support black owned businesses that I run into. Putting money into their business or even giving a shout out on social media can help their business grow. If black excellence was more talked about, more people would support it and black excellence would be more known and talked about. Even in schools, we will take time to notice things we haven't even talked about thanks to the research school provides for us.

Anyone can show support for black excellence by helping out with the black community, sharing and giving to the community. Any race can benefit from learning about black excellence because it can encourage them and also make them aware about some awesome people in the black excellence community. I think it should be taught in every subject, not just history. There are a lot of people in the world who helped out and did great things but didn't get to make it in the history book.

-Idreanna Graham

Black Excellence to
Idreanna Graham

My definition of black excellence is somebody who is African American and helps with the black community, where they are a model for both kids and adults. Black excellence is also when an African American is famous or getting to be famous and is giving back to their community and being a role model. Anyone can show support for black excellence by helping out with the black community, sharing and giving to the community. Any race can benefit from learning about black excellence because it can encourage them and also make them aware about some awesome people in the black excellence community. I think it should be taught in every subject, not just history. There are a lot of people in the world who helped out and did great things but didn't get to make it in the history book.

A prime example is my Aunt Kareemah Graham, who is an Management Analyst for the Department of Energy headquarters. Since she was 13 she has been employed. A couple of years ago she had a major setback. My aunt went unemployed for almost 2 years. This was all new to her and challenging but overall it was uplifting.It helped her complete her goals and made her stronger. My Aunt is an example of Black Excellence because she is a successful woman and has a plan to help young women and men. She's planning to give back to her community and family. My Aunt is planning to build a program for young men and women to help them get a job and to have a support system. My Aunt makes sure that the kids in the family always have a good time and have somebody to talk to or depend on. I couldn't ask for anybody else, my aunt is my role model!

Kelly Miller Smith is somebody who I think represents black excellence and I would like to learn more about him. I would like to learn about the things he did in his lifetime and what led up to him becoming a Baptist preacher, author, and prominent activist in the Civil Rights Movement. He went to Morehouse College and Howard University, he majored in divinity. Kelly Miller Smith represents black excellence because he spoke up for the black community. He was making social change. He was helping by leading and inspiring counter sit-ins, school desegregation and organizing the civil rights movement.

I'm planning to support black excellence by buying things made from black owned businesses and sharing it with social media. I think it's important to support black owned businesses to show my support and to get the word out there about unique and different things that are being made and not getting notice. I plan to eventually give back to my community. As of now I'm working with Martha's Table to give out food to the homeless. I want to encourage others the same way I've gotten encouraged by the black excellence community.

In conclusion, schools would change if we celebrated black excellence by making more kids have faith and look up to somebody. It can show us that just because where we are now doesn't mean we are going to be stuck here through the next 10 to 20 years. It shows that we can make a name for ourselves. It also shows that there are people out there who don't know us but are supporting and fighting for us, giving back and trying to help us.

Black Excellence Project
Jabari Matthews

It is important to learn black excellence because it shows that people of color have done things worth being noticed in history and that we are equal to everyone else. I think it is important to learn black excellence in school so kids learn from an early age to respect everyone no matter their race, religion, or sexuality. People are often not taught specifically about the achievements of people of color so learning it in schools is a good way to represent us people of color in a good way in order to break down the stereotypes. Other than school I learn black excellence by people's example in how they go through their everyday life of providing for their children and working to better the community.

I learn about black excellence in school by getting taught about people of color who have made a difference in the world which bettered the community and the image of people of color. I feel like black excellence should be taught more in detail in certain subjects but in every subject, there should be a little coverage on black excellence. In math and science, I expect to learn about black mathematicians and black scientists who made an impact in their communities that are still used to this day or have been used for a long period of time.

The most significant aspect of being a physician is that it helps the community in health, economics, technology and things such as that. In Charles R. Drew's field of work, he specifically helped people's health by focusing on blood preservation which is the study of keeping blood stored overtime and it still being ready for transfusion. He attended Amherst College in Massachusetts which was where he taught biology before going to McGill University and getting his MD degree in 1933, which then allowed him to become an instructor in surgery and an assistant surgeon at Freedman's hospital. This was the start of his career being a physician who studies blood preservation. Charles Drew used his career to fight racism by setting an example for the black community and showing them that they can be great too and that the racism, the judgment, and the unjust treatment cannot keep them bound up unless they allow it to. Also, as a form of fighting racism, Charles Drew argued that authorities should stop excluding the blood of African Americans from plasma-supply networks. However, after the armed forces ruled in 1942 that the blood of African-Americans would be accepted but would have to be stored separately from that of whites, Drew resigned his official posts, which was his way of standing up for what he believed in. Charles R. Drew shows black excellence by showing the world that black people can make a difference too and he did that by saving the lives of both black and white people equally.

Martin Luther King Jr. was a big example of black excellence because of how he stood up for people of color and how he spread the message of how black people are equal to white people and that they should be treated as such, he brought people of color together in order to fight against the injustice that keeps them under the white people who put themselves on a pedestal. I would like to learn about black activists who put their wellbeing on the line in order to help a community rise from their unfavorable place in society. Martin Luther King Jr. was an example of black excellence because he fought for the rights of other people without having any underlying meaning other than to help his people.

I show black excellence by being my best self in order to show how we people of color are hardworking and are images of excellence and are just as deserving of representation and praise as white people. Life would change if we showed black excellence because people would begin to break down and ignore the stereotypes placed on people of color.

My Black Excellence (Project)
Jalynn Stubbs

My definition of Black excellence is someone who helps other people and empowers them. Someone who fights for their rights, helps out their community, and tells the truth about our history. Someone who is a soldier, a tenacious person, and has a judicious mindset. A person who knows what they believe, fights for it, and doesn't regret empowerment but loves it. Everyone can show black excellence by fighting for what they believe while doing something that benefits their community. Such a person knows something is better for everyone and knows doing it will have consequences but still does it. People also should acknowledge other people who show black excellence, and if they don't know they have it themselves, they should be very proud when someone else acknowledges it in them. They have to be proud of who they are as a person and influence other people in a good way.

Learning black excellence will make people have a new way of thinking. Black excellence will determine people's actions/choices, but also black excellence will help determine who you really are as a person. People will experience a change in how they see life and change themselves from this. Someone from any race would benefit from learning about Black Excellence because Black Excellence will help you in some creative ways and inspiring ways. Black Excellence will help you in life and in your education, so learn it and use it. With math and science we could talk about famous people as well as less-known people who showed black excellence. Math and science should try to incorporate people who showed black excellence in their math and science classes so kids can learn new things in classes. So not just the students will be inspired but all people will. People will learn from these role models and learn new ways.

Someone who shows black excellence is my grandfather Joe L. Byrd. He is the father of two kids, the granddad and great granddad to over 10 kids, and also the brother of three other siblings. Joe L. Byrd was born on November 11,1948. My granddad was born in a little town in Oklahoma named Wewoka in Seminole County with his mother and his three siblings". They were there until they moved to Wichita. My granddad worked as a pipe fitter as a trade for 45 years, so first he did an apprenticeship and then became a journeyman. But Joe Byrd was also in the military and fought in the Vietnam War. My grandad shows black excellence based on how he views the world and tries to help me and my other family members to listen and learn from him. He says, "keep your family, always give that thought, you ain't nothing without family. To always be loved by your family, especially a black family, if we stand together, we together." My grandfather is smart and knows that black excellence means love and family. Those are the two things he cherishes and teaches us to cherish. But one more thing he wants us to do is do anything we put our mind to. He wants us to know how great we are, and he wants us to strive to be different from everyone. Joe L. Byrd's life is wonderful and I love him. He reflects who he really is even when he tries to hide it and this is my grandfather's history, I love learning so much more about it.

To me everyone can demonstrate black excellence if they show it or have it within them. But someone to me who shows a tremendous amount of black excellence is Taraji P. Henson. Taraji P. Henson worked hard to get to where she is and I relate to her since she is from where I'm from. Taraji P. Henson has about 4 awards but some people think for some famous people they just become famous, just like that. But Taraji P. henson worked as a secretary at the Pentagon in the mornings and as a singing-dancing waitress on a dinner-cruise ship, the ship name was the Spirit of Washington. She did this to pay for her college at Howard University and she studied drama. Taraji P. Henson is showing how it takes work to get to where you want to go and how you can achieve your goals with all the hard work you do. This is black excellence. She is ambitious, she inspires other people to be great, and she is a very authentic person. The key from learning from her is knowing what to do to succeed the normal way. It matters to learn from her because you're learning that you don't have to be from a known area or spot to become famous. Taraji P. Henson is enlightening me of how more of an amazing person I can be if I try and work towards my goals, not procrastinate. Taraji P. Henson has influenced me a lot, so I will learn from her, learn about more of the black excellence she shows, and one day become great like her.

A lot of people don't know what black excellence is but I give all my moral support to it. I will show my moral support by encouraging and agreeing with people who show the beautiful power of black excellence. I will help people who need help acknowledging what black excellence is and helping people acknowledge that blakc excellence is within them. Informing people on the importance of black excellence will make people believe more in it and give them more strength for anything that commences with them. Black excellence should be valued more, so I will show my purport towards black excellence by praising or giving back to the people who show black excellence. I will do all these things to show how foremost black excellence is all together.

Black excellence is what is really important to you. Black excellence is your own interpretation of expectations that you want to follow and what others to follow. But for you to have black excellence you have to not doubt yourself and believe in you or others too. So if you praise and believe in black excellence you should do things you believe shows black excellence, talk to people you believe show black excellence or become friends, and you can interview some people too. Black excellence is beautiful but you have to make the effects to achieve what you seek or what to learn from black excellence. So black excellence can be different from others but it can show in all.

Witnessing Black Excellence
Bailey M. Wiley

Black Excellence to me is when a person of the African American race is not only making their way toward success but also trying to better the community and make a positive change that will last for generations. It is important to learn about Black Excellence everywhere, because while someone is learning they will first see the struggle black people went through but still see how we as a whole have paved though all that hardship for future generations to be even better. This is so crucial because African Americans have a specific stigma towards them as some "ruthless" or a "ghetto" race. That's not the case so we try to do things for the community in order to remove the stigma placed on us. That's another reason why I feel as though Black Excellence should be incorporated in all subjects. In some way, shape or form, African American people have done something extraordinary in every subject. For instance, we have George Washington Carver who made many different items out of peanuts, Benjamin Banneker having no formal education but who acquired knowledge in math and history on his own, and even Madam C.J. Walker who was a self-made BLACK woman who made hair products. They are among the many who sparked Black Excellence.

Jeralyn Napper is a Pre-K 3 teacher but became a teacher of 3 year olds about 2 years ago. She faced many hardships to get to the place she is at today. Ms. Napper had her first child at the age of 17 and not only did she have her child but she was a single mother, moreover a BLACK single mother. She said that "It was a moment where many folks counted not only me, but also my child out. While it was heartbreaking, it also ignited a fire in me to 'prove them wrong' and dismantle the stereotype that exists surrounding teenage motherhood." This not only is a showing of Black excellence but also a showing of a person who wanted to let the world know that teenage mothers can make it too. Even though being a teenage mother was difficult she pulled through, her life was on track, and she even worked a regular corporate 9 to 5 job. But everything made a turn when Ms. Napper turned 26. She was diagnosed with an illness called fibromyalgia and that left her with a permanent disability that can impact her day to day life at any moment. She is an example of black excellence because even though all her hardships--being a teenage mother, being diagnosed with this illness took some toll on her life--she makes the best of it everyday. She went from working a 9 to 5 to teaching Pre-k 3 but not just any pre-k 3 group of kids, the kids in SE DC. She said that "I could not only provide highly engaging and rigorous instruction, but I could also promote civic leadership at the foundational level, in hopes of inspiring my students, as young as 3, to become advocates and change agents for their personal lives and the needs of their community." That to me is Black excellence in its greatest form.

One person I would like to learn more about would be former First Lady Michelle Obama. Mrs. Obama is a representation of Black Excellence not only for me but also many other Black women out there as well. Alongside former President Barack Obama being the first African American president, she was the First African American to become the First lady; that's a real game changer for the black community. On top of being the first black First Lady, Michelle is also an attorney! She has her own memoir out from a few years back, *Becoming*. It discusses her life for a global audience, from the very beginning (her roots), to personal experiences, her place as a mom, and time in the White House. Seeing Mrs. Obama doing this makes me believe that anyone, even African Americans and African American women, have the opportunity to succeed in life, you just have to want it bad enough. This goes to show that you can be the change and inspire the change you would want to see in your community and even across the world.

Black Excellence means a lot to me. I will always be for Black Excellence as a young African American female. I will support Black Excellence by speaking out for the community and making a positive change in the community by being like Ms. Napper and former First Lady Michelle Obama, making a way for other people to soon see that it is possible to be successful while being black. One thing I feel I do to support Black Excellence is by having my business, for which the whole goal is to motivate African Americans to love themselves because we were born black for a reason. Lastly, I have this one goal that is to actually get my business out there and do what I hope it would do. This is a goal of mine so that Black Excellence will always be shown though me as long as I'm alive.

Overall, I believe that if Black Excellence was experienced in day to day life, school and life would change significantly. I feel like school would change by finally having kids of all races but most importantly African American students learn about the positive side of their heritage instead of the trauma that their ancestors were put through every school year over and over again. For life, I think the stigma may lessen on African Americans. They will stop being seen as criminals just by the color of their skin, and the type of clothes they wear. They may finally get the life of having a FAIR trial like every other U.S citizen. In general, incorporating Black Excellence into life and school, would not only benefit the world and community but also have people feeling that we are one step closer to realizing that black people weren't the "founders" of American but did contribute a lot to getting it to the place it is today.

Khamara Ford

What black excellence means to me is when a black person has made themselves established enough in their community. When I say established I mean that the person has done something to improve or better their community. Trying to better your community can be shown in so many so many different ways such as giving back to those you love most, hosting fundraisers or giving snacks to the kids. To me black excellence also means when someone is brave enough to stand up in what they believe in and pursue their passion. It is important to learn about black excellence because the people that have already shown their black excellence could be your inspiration and inspire you to do the same thing they did.

Someone I would say is an example of black excellence is Chuck Brown. Chuck Brown is a musical artist who inspired many other people. He wanted to create his own significant sound that many people would grow to love. Before he started to blow up in music, he had a really tough early life. When Chuck Brown was only 15 he started living on the streets by himself. He quit school and did not get to graduate high school. He then went to jail for aggravated assault and while in jail he traded cigarettes for a guitar. When he got out he started to perform at parties in the area. He then joined a band called "Earls of Rhythm" and his career took off from there. Throughout his career he was fighting racism because in his music career he constantly got criticized about his music, they told him that his music wasn't good and it wouldn't blow up and no one would like it. He is an example of black excellence because he did not let other people's opinions affect how he felt about his music.

Someone else I think is an example of black excellence is Marvin Gaye. Marvin Gaye Was a singer, songwriter, and a record producer. He was one of the cofounders of Motown. In 1942 he won his first two grammy's from his album Midnight Love. In Gaye's early life he was born in washington d.c where he grew up in the area "simple city". When Gaye attended Randell junior high school he decided to take singing more seriously and join the glee club. Marvin Gayes is an example of black excellence because he made a name for himself and did not let his past affect who he wanted to become.

I will show my support for black excellences by always honoring the people that came before me and showing their black excellence. For example Taraji P. Henson and Samuel L. Jackson and Sharon Pratt. I feel like we should always look up to or pay respect to those that came before us and made it so we can do the things that we do today. For example, thanks to people like Moses Fleetwood Walker breaking the way people thought about black people playing sports, other black people who saw him had enough confidence to play.

I think it would be a great idea if schools started to teach about black excellence. I think if schools taught about black excellence kids would start to appreciate our black leaders a lot more. They should teach about all the people that made the world how it is today and all the ways black people made an impact on the whole world. I believe that kids should know all the people that came before them and how they started their careers and maybe if they learned about how that person became who they are it can influence how they could start their careers.

Black Excellence
Lily Thornton

I describe Black Excellence as an individual or group of individuals who possess honorable traits and abilities that allow the African American community to redefine what it means to be black in a systematically racist country. They do so by positive influence, professionalism, and educating the youth. Any person regardless of race can advocate for Black Excellence simply by not discrediting African Americans, and their ideas. Typically, in many history classes, we don't acquire knowledge about the inventions, art, or music that were created by black individuals. More often than not, we learn about previous ideals that were made by a person of color, that were further adapted by white people, then are later projected as their own ideas. This causes me to believe that all races can benefit from learning about Black Excellence and its significance because it can further push the idea of integrity into the American education system.

A figure who is an example of Black Excellence is DC Native, Jason Reynolds is a well-known African American literature artist that advocates for black youth. Similar to many children in the DMV area, Reynold's wasn't very fond of reading books in his early years. He was more interested in rap and writing poetry, and he didn't read his first novel fully until the age of seventeen. His most popular book series is called "Ghost" which is about a middle schooler, who is a student-athlete. He struggles with home life, because of his father's alcoholism. This alone shows a work of excellence because it covers real-life events. He has won many awards including the National Ambassador for Young People's Literature (Library of Congress), Walter Dean Myers Award, which is given to authors' who create diversity into their works, and the NAACP Award which is awarded to those who present African-American characters and culture through books, films, and literature. One of his works include a novel called "Stamped: Racism, Anti Racism, and You" which primarily focuses on the history of racism in the United States, and the hope of a future without racial hate. Also directed at children, this book provides the youth an opportunity to learn about social injustices, and educate them early on.

Alain Locke was an educator, philosopher, and writer. He was also was someone who thrived during the Harlem Rennassiance after making the term "New Negro" popular. This phrase was created to defy the Jim Crow segregation and practices. He studied in many great universities including Harvard University, Oxford, and University of Berlin. He also taught at HBCU Howard University. Locke's philosophy is called "cultural pluralism" which was the ability for the American people to be able to participate in an interconnected society despite cultural differences. He was the first black man to have been chosen to be a Rhodes scholar and created a book series called "Bronze Booklets of History, Problems, and Cultural Contributions of the Negro" He also was apart the LGBTQ community and supported many African American LGBTQ artists as well. However, after having difficulties for a few years, he died at the age of 69 from heart disease. I liked the idea of the "New Negro" movement, primarily because it redines the sterotypes, and popular beliefs on Black Americans. It also allows, us, to reclaim the term "negro" to regain that sense of power, from those who use it in a derogatory manner.

Through actively advocating for social justice reform and participation in youth summits, I demonstrate my support for Black Excellence. Not only is it vital for the acknowledgement of Black success in education, the idea of teaching and practicing it is equally as necessary.

Moving Forward.
Vanessa Anderson, Ph.D.
Founding Principal, Bard Early College, D.C.

As always, my students teach and inspire me. Thumbing through this year's edition of The Black Excellence Project, I am reminded of why Bard DC is such an amazing place. On a daily basis, our students ask and answer and re-examine questions such as, "What is Black excellence? Who embodies it? What is the school's role in fostering it?"

The last question strikes me as paramount. It is clear that we do have a role in how we center blackness, give students voice and make sure that representation is a priority in the classes we teach, how we choose to teach them and who gets access to and encouragement in those classes. But it is also important, as authors Ay'Maya Murchison and Samara Winston suggest, that we normalize Black achievement and not notions of Black criminality within our schools.

We have lived through a historic year. A year characterized by a global pandemic, the unmasking and forced confrontation of centuries of racialized brutality, and an unprecedented insurrection at the Capitol. We have also witnessed the election and inauguration of our first Black female Vice President and Georgia's first Black Senator, much of which was possible through the organizing efforts of another Black woman from Georgia. Black excellence? Absolutely. But as you all lived through this history, showing up, continuing to build our school community and make your voices heard in class, advisory, the literary magazine, school newspaper and student government, you embodied day-to-day excellence.

I'm also reminded, as I read London Haynie's essay of the importance of recognizing the excellence that is in the less heavy, less historic moments. The excellence, as her friend, Peyton describes it, of "surviving in a world that is against you, freely and happily." The world needs you all. As you pursue excellence in fields as varied as law, literature, mathematics, science, the arts and politics, please never lose sight of your right to live freely and happily.

Amateka College Prep
works with middle and high school students
to advance understanding of Black groups
in multiracial, multicultural communities.

To learn more, visit: www.AmatekaCollegePrep.org